POLITICS IN THE ANCIENT WORLD

Canto is a new imprint offering a range of
titles, classic and more recent, across a
broad spectrum of subject areas and
interests. History, literature, biography,
archaeology, politics, religion, psychology,
philosophy and science are all represented
in Canto's specially selected list of titles,
which now offers some of the best and
most accessible of Cambridge publishing to
a wider readership.

POLITICS IN
THE ANCIENT WORLD

M. I. FINLEY

*Professor Emeritus of Ancient History
and former Master of Darwin
College, Cambridge*

CAMBRIDGE
UNIVERSITY PRESS

Published by the Press Syndicate of the University of Cambridge
The Pitt Building, Trumpington Street, Cambridge CB2 1RP
40 West 20th Street, New York NY 10011-4211, USA
10 Stamford Road, Oakleigh, Melbourne 3166, Australia

First published 1983
Reprinted 1984 (twice, with corrections), 1987, 1989
Canto edition 1991, 1994

Printed in Malta at Interprint Limited

Library of Congress catalogue card number: 83 – 1771

British Library Cataloguing in Publication Data
Finley, M. I.
Politics in the ancient world.
1. Greece – Politics and government
2. Rome – Politics and government
I. Title
320.938   JC73

ISBN 0 521 40673 0 paperback

CONTENTS

TO
JOHN DUNN

PREFACE

This book has been built round the four Wiles Lectures that I had the honour to give at the Queen's University, Belfast, in May 1980. Four of the chapters are revised versions of those lectures, whereas chapters 2 and 6 were written afterwards and were first made public in a shorter form as a J. C. Jacobsen Memorial Lecture of the Royal Danish Academy of Sciences and Letters (and published in early 1982 in the Academy's *Meddelelser*).

The English word 'politics' has a semantic range that differs somewhat from that of its synonyms in other western languages. On the one hand, 'politics' is not normally employed in the sense of 'policy'; on the other hand, it has more of the implication of the ways, informal as much as formal, in which government is conducted and governmental decisions are arrived at, and of the accompanying ideology. Politics in that sense are essentially my theme.

I am unaware of any previous book-length account of my subject, with which I have been concerned and on which I have published a few articles over the past twenty-odd years. I have found the subject not an easy one, especially once I took the decision to discuss Greece and Rome comparatively, and I have not hesitated to draw on the knowledge and the thinking of friends and colleagues. My warm thanks go to them all, although I name only those who read and commented on the typescript of this book: Tony Andrewes, Peter Brunt, John Dunn, Peter Garnsey, Wilfried Nippel and Dick Whittaker. Further thanks are due, collectively though anonymously, to the colleagues, most of them from Belfast, historians and political scientists but few specialists in ancient history, who, as is the Wiles custom, were invited to participate each evening in a wide-ranging discussion of the day's lecture. And many more colleagues joined in the warm hospitality that marked the occasion, led by the Vice-Chancellor, Dr Peter Froggatt, and the representatives of the Wiles Trust, Professors Alan Astin and David Harkness.

Douglas Matthews kindly prepared the index.

My wife, finally, displayed her inexhaustible patience while I wrestled with yet another composition.

Darwin College, Cambridge   M. I. F.
September 1982

I
STATE, CLASS AND POWER

In the third book of the *Politics* (1279b6-40) Aristotle wrote: 'Tyranny is the rule of one man to the advantage of the ruler, oligarchy to the advantage of the rich, democracy to the advantage of the poor.' He then went on to gloss this definition: 'whether the few or the many rule is accidental to oligarchy and democracy – the rich are few everywhere, the poor many . . . The real difference between democracy and oligarchy is poverty and wealth.'

Late in the nineteenth century, in his great commentary on the *Politics*, W. L. Newman observed that Aristotle was here giving 'explicit recognition to an important truth', for the prevailing modern social-contract theory of the state 'obscures our recognition of the fact which Aristotle had long ago pointed out, that the constitution of a State has its roots in what moderns term its social system'.[1] More precisely, Aristotle gave systematic formulation to a common but still rather loose notion that was widely (perhaps universally) shared by the classical Greeks. It pervades their literature, among poets, historians and pamphleteers as well as political philosophers – from Hesiod's bitter complaint against the 'gift-devouring' princes and their crooked judgments, through the reformer Solon's boast, 'I stood covering both [rich and poor] with a strong shield, permitting neither to triumph unjustly over the other', to Plato's lengthy insistence that even before the degenerate present, the great Athenian leaders of the good old days, Miltiades, Themistocles, Cimon and Pericles, were no better than pastry-cooks, stuffing the common people (*demos*) with material goods.[2]

The ambiguity of the word *demos* is directly relevant: on the one hand, it meant the citizen-body as a whole, as in the opening words of the formal decrees of a democratic Greek assembly – 'the *demos* has decided'; on the other hand, it meant the common people, the

---

[1] W. L. Newman, *The Politics of Aristotle* (4 vols., Oxford 1887–1902) I 223.
[2] Hesiod, *Works and Days* 248–64; Solon as quoted by Aristotle, *Constitution of Athens* 12.1; Plato, *Gorgias* 502E–519D, respectively.

many, the poor, as in Plato's *Gorgias*.[3] The Latin *populus* had the same double connotation. Yet there was no uncertainty in the usage in any particular context: Greek and Roman writers and speakers shifted freely from one sense to the other with easy intelligibility, and, when they were being critical of democracy, they punned freely on *demos* or *populus*, with no less intelligibility. Both languages were also rich in euphemisms, Greek especially so – euphemisms that were as one-sided as the literature in which they occur. As substitutes for 'the rich', Greek writers employed words that meant literally 'the useful (or worthy)' (*chrestoi*), 'the best' (*beltistoi*), 'the powerful' (*dynatoi*), 'the notable' (*gnorimoi*), 'the well-born' (*gennaioi*); for 'the poor' they said 'the many' (*hoi polloi*), 'the mean' (*cheirones*), 'the knaves' (*poneroi*), 'the mob' (*ochlos*). In Latin, the *boni* or *optimi* stood against the *plebs*, the *multitudo*, the *improbi*.[4]

Euphemisms can of course also be ambivalent: in no small number of texts their literal sense overlaps and even overrides their figurative sense, as when Cicero complained, as he did frequently and in varied terms, that many *boni* were not behaving as *boni*. The fact remains, however, that more often than not 'rich' and 'poor' render the sense better than a literal translation. The language of ancient politics thus confirms Aristotle's 'important truth', that (no longer in Newman's formulation) the state is an arena for conflicting interests, conflicting classes. No Greek or Roman would have disputed that, no matter how often they said otherwise in political debates (not unlike their counterparts today). Greek political thinkers sought the ideal state in which conflict would be transcended in the interest of the good life for all, but they insisted that no actual states, past or present, attained or even approached that goal. Solon was no exception, despite his shield-metaphor, which he applied to himself personally, not to the Athenian state. He had been assigned the task of reforming Athens in order to reduce the power of the rich to act in their self-interest, and he claimed to have done so without transferring so much power to the poor that they in turn could act one-sidedly in *their* interest. He thus acknowledged the centrality of classes and class conflict.

[3] For the *testimonia*, see S. Cagnazzi in *Quaderni di storia* 11 (1980) 297–314.
[4] My lists are not complete. For Greek usage see briefly Loenen (1953) 7–10; for Latin in full, J. Hellegouarc'h, *Le vocabulaire latin des relations et des partis politiques sous la République* (Paris 1963) pt IV.

2

Yet, perhaps surprisingly at first sight, many modern commentators and historians seem hardly to have noticed what the Greeks and Romans were saying on the subject. The standard current studies of Aristotle's *Politics*, including the commentaries on Book III (Newman's among them), do not address themselves to the implications of the fundamental passage with which I began, repeated as a leitmotiv throughout the work.[5] Historians, concerned with the realities of ancient political behaviour rather than with concepts and theories, cannot similarly pretend that Newman's 'important truth' had no relevance; so they frequently adopt other evasive or dismissive devices. First they concede that in the bad old days of the archaic period, in both Greece and Rome, the aristocrats and patricians who monopolized power were greedy and nasty – but that, after all, was the formative, the 'pre-state' period. Then they treat the history of politics in the subsequent, classical period as largely one of decline and degeneration, particularly in those moments or periods when class interests were overtly active. 'These social conflicts', writes Victor Ehrenberg about classical Greece, 'which in many places ended by turning into party struggles, menaced the *polis* in its very existence as a community of citizens.'[6] Pejorative labels abound, some derived from ancient sources – demagogue, faction, the mob; others coined by the historians themselves, such as moderate and radical democracy.

Roman history is more troublesome, particularly the final century of the Republic, during (and about) which Roman orators and writers were so explicitly class-conscious that only the most blinkered modern historian can maintain total silence about class divisions. Positive action is required to abate the nuisance, and I shall consider two illustrations.

The first is what modern historians have come to call the *senatus consultum ultimum*, a resolution of the Senate implying that the state (*res publica*) was in danger and calling upon the magistrates to take all necessary defensive actions. The 'subversive' elements were then treated as enemies of the state, outlaws (and were sometimes formally declared to be such), *a fortiori* no longer entitled to the protection of the law, in particular to the right to a formal trial. The unambiguously attested instances, fewer than a dozen in all, fell

[5] Cf. *Politics* 1281a12–19, 1289b29–32, 1290a30–b20, 1291b2–13, 1296a22–32, 1296b24–34, 1315a31–33, 1317b2–10, 1318a31–32.
[6] Ehrenberg (1976) 154; cf. Spahn (1977) 25–6. See further below in ch. 5.

between 121 and 43 B.C., in other words, in the final century of the Republic, when, as we shall see, armed violence or the threat of armed intervention seriously distorted the substance of city-state politics. Many thousands of Romans were massacred under the several *senatus consulta ultima* in open violation of the long-standing procedures for the capital punishment of a citizen. Admittedly, Gaius Gracchus had occupied the Aventine with armed supporters in 121 B.C., and Saturninus in 100 and Catiline in 63 also led armed bands. However, Gaius Gracchus had behind him the experience of his brother Tiberius a decade earlier: Tiberius had been clubbed to death by a mob of senators and their retainers *when the consul refused to take 'emergency' measures and the Senate had not issued a 'final decree'.* It was not illogical for Gaius to believe that the ruling class, having lost confidence in its ability to rule by traditional methods, was prepared to find a new formula. That they did, by inventing the *senatus consultum ultimum.*

The volume of modern writing on the subject, overwhelmingly concerned with questions of constitutional law, tends to avoid the central issue of what can be meant by 'a threat to the safety of the state'.[7] The Gracchi were aiming at a tyranny – that became the conventional answer in the hostile ancient sources, and it is frequently repeated by modern historians.[8] The evidence for that charge is so flimsy, not to say non-existent, that it would be dismissed out of hand in a less ideologically weighted context.[9] Another ancient tradition surfaced in two later Greek writers, Plutarch and Appian, namely, that the struggle between the two brothers and the Senate was a phase in the continuing conflict between the rich and the poor (the precise terms they used). Mere 'chatter', Badian comments, 'which some scholars still take as valid evidence. It is no more than a stereotype of *stasis* – a purely literary device of little use to the historian.' The rich were not all that rich, he argues, and many poor were indifferent to, and increasingly disenchanted with, the Gracchan programme.[10] No doubt, but the

---

[7] For an excessively long, conventional account see Ungern-Sternberg (1970). Both the *senatus consultum* and the modern literature on the subject have been properly deflated by A. Guarino, 'Senatus consultum ultimum', in *Sein und Werden im Recht. Festgabe für Ulrich von Lübtow . . .*, ed. W. G. Becker and L. Schnorr von Carolsfeld (Berlin 1970), pp. 281–94.

[8] E.g. Badian (1972).

[9] Note the effort by Badian (1972) 722–6 to get round this weakness of his case.

[10] Badian (1972) 707, 716–20.

same can be said about any open clash between classes or interests throughout history. It remains the case that agrarian reform or the pressure of debt provided the occasion not only for the Gracchan 'state of emergency' but for several of the later *senatus consulta ultima*, and that, at the simplest level, the proposals disapproved by the Senate benefited (or would have benefited) poor citizens at the expense of rich citizens. And it also remains unchallenged that the Senate arrogated to itself the unqualified right to determine when a state of emergency existed of such gravity as to warrant the abrogation of the fundamental rights of Roman citizens; that the Senate, in short, identified itself with the *res publica*.

Of course the Senate, like all governmental organs or politicians ever since, insisted (and, I will concede, believed) that they were acting in the general interest, not in the interest of the rich or the oligarchy. 'The death of Tiberius Gracchus', wrote Cicero (*Republic* 1.19.31), 'and his whole conduct of the tribunate before that divided one people into two parts.' That was a judgment of extraordinary disingenuousness even by Ciceronian standards, but he did not flinch from its implications: Scipio Nasica, he said several times, performed a great service to the state when he killed Tiberius Gracchus though acting in a private capacity.[11] Occasional twinges of conscience in the governing circles are recorded, once by Cicero himself (*Against Catiline* 1.1.3), but only because the illegality of Scipio's action was so blatant. Few doubts were raised that the state was under threat – and those few for obviously partisan reasons – or that armed repression was called for or that the decision lay with the Senate.

The recorded Roman reactions are what we expect, given the structure of Roman government in the period and the nature of our sources. It is perhaps more surprising that modern historians, with few exceptions, share the 'official' Roman view so unreservedly.[12] Lintott concludes that 'in principle' the *senatus consultum ultimum* was 'a salutary institution', though in practice the 'attitude' of the magistrates who acted under its shield became 'a more arrogant and extremist' one 'which, often with justification, was easily suspected

[11] *De officiis* 1.22.76; *Tusculan Disputations* 4.23.51; *Oration on His House* 34.91.
[12] A notable exception is A. Guarino, in his review of Ungern-Sternberg (1970) in *Labeo* 18 (1972) 95–100: 'Il "Notstandsrecht des Senat" non è il "Notstandsrecht" della repubblica' (p. 96). See also R. E. Smith, 'The Anatomy of Force in Late Republican Politics', in Badian (1966) 257–73.

of being partisan'.[13] That is a strange way of saying that the 'salutary institution' was regularly used to preserve the power of the governing class. Another historian closes his account by quoting Cicero's defence of his own action in putting the Catilinarians to death – I acted 'with the authority (*auctoritas*) of the Senate and the general consent of all *boni*' (*Oration on His House* 35.94) – and then comments that, though the use of the word *boni* gives the remark a 'strong Optimate colouring', nevertheless 'public opinion' was a necessary condition for the enforcement of a *senatus consultum ultimum*: 'for the Senate and the people as for the magistrates, even in a state of emergency (and indeed precisely then) the decisive guide-line must be, Salus populi suprema lex esto.'[14]

My present concern is not with the evaluation of the gravity of the Gracchan crises or of any of the other situations in which comparable repressive action was taken, but with the conception of the state implicit in the approach I have exemplified, and in particular with the rejection of the Aristotelian 'important truth' about it.[15] The second illustration I promised, which is from the study of Roman civil procedure, has been chosen with the same concern in mind.

In 1966 J. M. Kelly published a book, *Roman Litigation*, composed, in the words of a reviewer, 'around a single thesis: this is that, despite the ideal of justice expressed in sources from Cicero to Justinian, the procedures and operation of the law clearly reflected the harsh realities of Roman society, and failed to mitigate the difference between rich and poor'.[16] Remarkably, we had to wait until 1966 for the first full-scale study ever undertaken of the actual functioning of the Roman law of civil procedure. No less remarkably, some who gave the book a friendly reception went to considerable lengths to reduce its significance almost to triviality. I refer not to their deployment of the standard deflating devices – 'the case has, no doubt, a good deal of cumulative weight' but the 'central thesis is overstated', or 'I nevertheless believe' (the normal sign of 'I have no refuting evidence') – but to their concentration on

---

[13] Lintott (1968) 173.

[14] Ungern-Sternberg (1970) 131. The quotation is from Cicero, *Laws* 3.3.8: 'The safety of the people shall be the highest law.'

[15] Throwaway concessions that are then ignored in the analysis do not warrant any qualification of my reference to rejection; e.g. Badian (1972) 716: 'It was true, of course, that the centuriate assembly was weighted in favour of the prosperous.'

[16] M. W. Frederiksen, in *Journal of Roman Studies* 57 (1967) 254.

dishonesty and corruption in the administration of the law. In an amusing variation, Max Kaser did not mind corruption among the magistrates so long as one conceded the moral purity of the jurists.[17] But that is not what Kelly's book is chiefly about. Crook and Stone went to the heart of the matter when they distinguished two questions: '(a) is the law administered impartially?, and (b) is the mould of the law itself – the set of rules, including those of procedure – an instrument and reflection of social inequality?'.[18] The answer to their second question seems to me to be a commonplace: of course the 'mould' of Roman law, as of every other legal system examined by historians, was an instrument and a reflection of society and therefore of social inequality. Probably few historians would deny that, if challenged directly, unlike those students of Roman law who applaud the Roman jurists for their 'instinctive dread of a syncretism of the economic and juristic methods'.[19] But few historians seem to be challenged (or to challenge themselves) often enough; they are generally happy to consider only the first question posed by Crook and Stone and to remain within the limitless field of corruption and maladministration. Tacitly they thus contribute to the survival of the old mystique about the law as something that stands above and outside society and its realities, with its own essence, its autonomous logic, its independent existence. And so, too, with the state. 'It was Wilamowitz', we are told in Ehrenberg's standard work on the Greek state, 'who clearly recognized that oligarchy and democracy are nothing but variants of the same type of state, which is characterized by the "sovereignty" of the citizen with full rights.' This turns out to mean no more than that the 'true' Greek *polis* was not a monarchy,[20] and I submit that a taxonomy that reduces all states to two types, one in

---

[17] M. Kaser, in *Zeitschrift der Savigny-Stiftung für Rechtsgeschichte, Romanistische Abteilung* 84 (1967) 521.

[18] In their review of Kelly (1966) in *Classical Review*, n.s. 17 (1967) 83–6; cf. the review by G. I. Luzzatto in *Studia et documenta historiae et iuris* 32 (1966) 377–84, and R. Villers, 'Le droit romain, droit d'inégalité', *Revue des études latines* 47 (1969) 462–81.

[19] Lübtow (1948) 475. This book-length article by a reputed Romanist is a *reductio ad absurdum* of what is still the prevailing view. Thus F. Schulz, *Principles of Roman Law*, trans. M. Wolff (Oxford 1936), p. 24, writes (cited by Lübtow): Roman 'legal writings ignore the genetic connection between law and extra-legal matters . . . No economic considerations enter into the law.' The illegitimate shift from what jurists say to the mould of the law itself is apparent.

[20] Ehrenberg (1976) 97 and 87, respectively.

which sovereignty resides in one man, the other in which sovereignty resides in the 'citizens' however they may be defined, is of no analytical utility. Worse still, the notion that a state can be characterized – one might almost say defined – by the sovereignty of the citizen with full rights is only a short step from the nonsense of 'das römische Volk ist der römische Staat' (the Roman people is the Roman state).[21] This is not the place for a theoretical account of the state. For my purposes it is sufficient to enunciate some elementary and obvious postulates. The first is that in a study of politics there is no meaningful distinction between state and government. Political metaphysicians notwithstanding, the citizens (or subjects) in any regime equate the two, even in a revolutionary situation. As was well said in a book that I suppose no one reads any longer, Harold Laski's *The State in Theory and Practice*,

the citizen can reach his state only through the government . . . He infers . . . the nature of the state from the character of its governmental acts; and he cannot know it otherwise. That is why no theory of the state is adequate that does not make the governmental act central to the explanation it offers. A state is what its government does; what any given theory requires that government should do to fulfil the ideal purpose of the state is merely . . . a criterion for judging it and not an index to its actual essence.[22]

This was all the more true of antiquity: then the citizen's personal contacts were directly with the government – the legislators, the executive, the courts – because there was no mediating bureaucracy.

Government, the state, implies power both internally and externally – that is my second postulate, and I am not immediately concerned (as I shall be later) to distinguish power in its sense of *potestas* from power in its sense of *auctoritas*. Power is more than coercion, but state power is unique, overriding all other 'powers' within the society by its acknowledged right to exercise force, even to kill, when its representatives deem such action to be necessary (and also legitimate where the rule of law prevails). Such a formulation will no doubt be dismissed as simple-minded by the political scientists and sociologists who are responsible for much current writing about power, which in effect dissolves the notion

---

[21] Lübtow (1948) 481.   [22] Laski (1935) 57–8.

8

into dust.[23] And it will be rejected by those anthropologists who demand a 'culture-free view' that allows for political organizations in which political decisions are not 'binding on the society' and for 'political units without governmental apparatus'.[24] However, I believe that few others will find much difficulty in understanding or accepting my second postulate, and I shall concern myself with the manifestations of state power in the ancient world, not with formal definition.

The third simple postulate is that the choice of those who govern and the ways in which they govern depend on the structure of the particular society under examination. A central feature of the societies with which we are concerned was the important presence of slaves; another was the severe restriction among the Greeks of access to citizenship; a third was the exclusion of women from any direct participation in political or governmental activity. The view is therefore frequently echoed that it is wrong to speak of democracy, rights or freedom at any time in ancient history. That seems to me to misconceive the nature of historical inquiry, to reduce it to a game of awarding credits and demerits according to the historian's own value-system. Moral condemnation, no matter how well-founded, is no substitute for historical or social analysis. 'Rule by the few' or 'rule by the many' was a meaningful choice, the freedom and the rights that the factions claimed for themselves were worth fighting for, despite the fact that even 'the many' were a minority of the whole population.[25]

Thus far, I have deliberately spoken of Aristotle's (or Newman's) 'important truth' and employed his terminology as a counter to the current bad habit of pinning the Marxist label on any and every

---

[23] See, e.g., the references in S. Lukes, *Power: A Radical View* (London 1974).

[24] W. W. Tiffany, in *Political Anthropology*, ed. S. L. Seaton and H. J. M. Claessen (The Hague 1975), pp. 70 and 65, and M. Gluckman, *Politics, Law and Ritual in Tribal Society* (Oxford 1965), p. 84, respectively. (I have deliberately selected examples other than those criticized in Finley (1975) 113-15.) For an effective rebuttal by an anthropologist, see the opening pages of M. C. Webb, 'The Flag Follows Trade . . .', in *Ancient Civilization and Trade*, ed. J. A. Sabloff and C. C. Lamberg-Karlovsky (Albuquerque 1975), pp. 155-209; cf. W. G. Runciman, 'Origins of States: The Case of Archaic Greece', *Comparative Studies in Society and History* 24 (1982) 351-77.

[25] It is absurdly necessary for an ancient historian to say explicitly that he will not be denied such good English words as 'faction' or 'client'. It is pedantry to object because the Latin *factio* and *cliens* are technical terms with different nuances from the modern.

9

political analysis that employs a concept of class,[26] a habit that ignores the long history of such an approach, in one form or another, in western political analysis ever since Aristotle.[27] I have also used the term 'class' loosely, as we customarily do in ordinary discourse. Aristotle's 'rich' and 'poor' were such classes, undefined but nevertheless identifiable by contemporaries.[28] The poor embraced all the free men who laboured for their livelihood, the peasants who owned their farms as well as the tenants, the landless labourers, the self-employed artisans, the shopkeepers. They were distinguished on the one hand from the 'rich', who were able to live comfortably on the labour of others, but also from the paupers, the beggars, the idlers.[29] Obviously a simple binary classification cannot be pushed to mean more than it does, particularly not to be converted into a sociologically acceptable class structure. Aristotle himself sometimes broke it down further in specific contexts and referred to farmers or herders or craftsmen. Occasionally he also showed a fondness for *to meson*, the middle, but then he was merely reflecting his well-known doctrine, central to his biological and ethical works, that the mean is natural, the best, whereas excess in either direction is a disorder.[30] In the *Politics*, *to meson* appears only in a few normative generalizations – 'The larger *poleis* are more free from civil disturbance (*stasis*) because *to meson* is numerous' – of little practical significance, for 'in most states *to meson* is small' (1296a9-24).[31]

---

[26] It is sufficient to cite R. Sealey's statement that the 'Marxist account of Athenian political conflicts' has been 'given in classic form' by Beloch and de Ste Croix: 'The Entry of Pericles into History', *Hermes* 84 (1956) 234-47, at p. 242. The latter has now turned Aristotle into a Marxist: *The Class Struggle in the Ancient Greek World* (London 1981), pp. 69–80.

[27] See Hintze (1962) 425–6, in an essay originally published in 1913 by an outstanding German political historian, who untypically for his time was deeply concerned with the significance of Marxist views.

[28] See Nippel (1980) 103–5.

[29] See Finley (1973a) 40–2, with bibliography. In that book I argued that 'status' and 'order' are preferable to 'class' in analysing the ancient economy. My return in the present work to 'class' (in the sense intended in ordinary discourse, not in a technical sense, Marxist or other) does not imply a change of view. I merely find the conventional terminology more convenient, and harmless, in an account of ancient politics.

[30] See S. R. L. Clark, *Aristotle's Man* (Oxford 1975), pp. 84–97.

[31] We read in the *Politics* (1289b28-32) that there are three classes, the rich, the poor and the middle, with the rich possessing hoplite equipment, the poor not. Such inconsequence, with no place in the qualifying condition (hoplite equipment) for

We must therefore restrict ourselves to the ancient connotations of the word-pair, rich and poor, and we must sedulously avoid the modern corollary of a substantial middle class with its own defined interests. Although the ancient classes and sub-classes did not regularly, or even often, think or act collectively as one class in conflict with others, most notably not when questions of war and empire were at issue, there were times when enough of them or a particular segment did. Then, the unfailing schematic formulation by ancient writers was that the *polis* had been split into two contending classes, not three. In democracies, Aristotle generalized disapprovingly (*Politics* 1310a3-10), 'demagogues are always dividing the *polis* into two, waging war against the rich', while there are oligarchic states in which the oligarchs swear, 'I shall be ill-disposed to the *demos* and plan whatever evil I can against them.' That exemplifies class, class consciousness and class conflict sufficiently for my purposes. More concreteness and specificity will emerge as the analysis proceeds.

I have shifted, more or less casually so far, between Greece and Rome. The casualness will disappear, but the very possibility of incorporating Greece and Rome into a single discourse has earlier been challenged (with reference to my *Ancient Economy*) and I must make some acknowledgement of the opposition.[32] My present subject is politics, and specifically city-state politics.[33] For reasons to be considered at the beginning of the third chapter, my sole concern is with the self-governing city-state, or at times with what pretended to be a city-state (excluding not only the monarchies but also the Greek tyrannies).[34] That means the Greek world from the

the middle class, is remarkable for Aristotle, and helps confirm my judgment that he occasionally injected the doctrine of the mean into this work quite mechanically and quickly put it aside in his own account. I stress the point chiefly because Christian Meier (1980) has pivoted his analysis of Greek political development round this, on my view fictitious, middle class (see briefly n. 48 in ch. 2 below), an analysis expanded at length by his pupil Spahn (1977).

[32] E.g. J. Andreau, 'M. I. Finley, la banque antique et l'économie moderne', *Annali . . . Pisa*, 3rd ser., 7 (1977) 1129–52.

[33] 'City-state' is not a very good translation of the Greek *polis* but it is conventional and also convenient in permitting the inclusion of Rome, for which *polis* is inappropriate.

[34] The reason for excluding monarchies will be made clear early in ch. 3. Tyrants are excluded because they made no effort to institutionalize their position and remained 'outside the fabric of the *polis*': D. Lanza, *Il tiranno e il suo pubblico* (Turin 1977), pp. 163–4.

late archaic period, say the mid-seventh century, to the conquests by Alexander the Great or a little later; the Roman world from the mid-fifth century B.C. to the late Republic. No one need be puzzled by the departure from the conventional periodization of either Greek or Roman history, an artificial frame (especially in Greek history) that is inappropriate for the analysis of several important aspects of ancient society.[35]

The very label 'city-state' implies the existence of common elements sufficient to justify taking Greece and Rome together, at least as a point of departure. But there were also important differences as early as the time when the first historical record emerges from legendary prehistory and a growing divergence thereafter, especially once Roman conquest and expansion began to weaken the city-state frame. The single label 'ancient' does not imply identity either among different regions or peoples or over long periods of time. It is enough to contrast Athens and Sparta or pre-Cleisthenic and post-Periclean Athens within the Greek world. As we proceed, major variations will emerge alongside substantial continuities, and they are more clearly visible and meaningful from a Graeco-Roman comparison than from a narrowing of the field of observation to one or the other. That, after all, is what Dionysius of Halicarnassus did in his *Roman Antiquities* (5.65.1) when he had a fifth-century B.C. Roman call on the Senate to learn from Solon; or Cicero when he wrote his *Republic* and *Laws* on the 'model' of Plato.

At the beginning of our story, the social structure was notably alike in the Greek city-states and in Rome: they were agrarian societies, in which the open class conflicts, so central in archaic Greek and Roman history, were regularly and exclusively between landed aristocratic creditors and peasant debtors.[36] Power, authority, was monopolized by the former, both formally and *de facto*. 'Aristocracy' is yet another ambiguous word, but we are here faced with an estate or order in a strict sense, families that so identified themselves and were so acknowledged by the others; most clearly in Rome with the emergence (which we can no longer trace) of a closed patrician order; less certainly in Greece, perhaps only

---

[35] See Finley (1975) 64–6 on the lack of synchronization between Roman legal history and the conventional periods.

[36] Weber (1972) 797–8 stresses the contrast in this respect with the medieval communes.

because of the nature of the evidence, though we should not underestimate the regular claim of 'heroic' or divine ancestors as a pointer. They also possessed much of the wealth; the modern tendency to denigrate that on grounds of scale must be resisted. Wealth is always a relative concept; what matters is that archaic Greek and Roman aristocrats controlled enough resources and manpower (also an element of wealth) to acquire weaponry and horses for themselves, to be able to import metals and other necessities and sometimes to provide the requisite shipping, to construct stone temples and other public works. The legend of the haughty aristocrat Cincinnatus summoned from his plough on his 2½-acre farm (four *iugera*) in 458 B.C. in order to rescue Rome from military peril (Livy 3.26.7-12), tells us something about later Roman ideology (as the absence of such tales among the Greeks informs us about their different ideology). On the realities of fifth-century Rome the legend serves only to mislead badly.

Some aristocrats had no doubt managed to become impoverished; more important, a number of outsiders acquired enough wealth to feel themselves entitled to share in the monopoly of power. The process may be wholly mysterious to us but not the consequences, thanks to several indicators. In Athens, for example, Solon in 594 B.C. divided the citizenry into four wealth categories for various purposes, including eligibility for public office. Formally that marked a complete break with the exclusive rights of a hereditary order, of a nobility of birth, though the aristocratic families continued to predominate in the new wealth-determined ruling class, at least for some time. Two points are worth noticing: (1) the qualification for each of the four Solonic 'classes' was defined solely in terms of agricultural yield; (2) three of the 'classes' retained traditional labels, *hippeis, zeugitai, thetes,* but the members of the fourth and highest category were called *pentakosiomedimnoi* (five-hundred-bushelmen), a blatantly artificial coinage that symbolizes the timocratic quality of the scheme.

In Rome, too, the timocratic principle was introduced into the governmental (and military) system at a roughly comparable stage, and became so firmly entrenched that Nicolet has rightly labelled Rome a *cité censitaire*.[37] For the first phase, the evidence about the

[37] Nicolet (1976).

details, all of it late and filled with anachronisms, seems to me to be corrupt beyond redemption.[38] However, there can be no doubt about the entry of non-patricians into the higher offices step by step (beginning with the office of 'military tribune with consular power') or of the concession of legitimacy to marriages between patricians and plebeians, traditionally in 445 B.C. Both firmly imply the existence of richer men among the plebeians (in technical language, all citizens who were not patricians). The Roman patriciate was a singularly inelastic order, open to outside recruits only by the formal adoption of an individual male into a patrician family, a solemn act requiring state approval. The archaic body of plebs therefore had to become an order, too, analogous to the medieval Italian *popolo*.[39]

So complete a dichotomy had no parallel in Greece – at least we have no evidence for anything like the plebeian order – but the distinction was anyway soon minimized in so far as practical politics were concerned. What matters in the present context is that, at the point at which we begin our inquiry, both the Roman plebeians and their counterparts in Greece, the bulk of the citizen-population, overwhelmingly rural, were already differentiated by wealth and status. In the ensuing centuries, not only did the gap between rich and poor widen greatly but there was also further diversification of the social structure. The tempo and range of development differed from city-state to city-state among the Greeks and most dramatically between them collectively and the Romans. The closed Roman patriciate was effectively displaced by a new aristocracy (*nobilitas*), which was not exclusively hereditary and never institutionalized as an 'estate' or 'order', incorporating 'new' lineages (*gentes*) of whom an increasing majority were plebeian in the old sense as the patrician families gradually died out.[40] Admission

---

[38] The discussion centres on the *comitia centuriata*. For a concise account of the *comitia* (conventional except for an aberrant section on a supposed, abortive industrial revolution at the end of the fourth century B.C.) see Staveley (1972) ch. 6; more discursive and wide-ranging, also more sceptical towards the late Roman sources, is Nicolet (1976) ch. 7; both provide sufficient bibliography. See also Nicolet, 'L'idéologie du système centuriate et l'influence de la philosophie politique grecque', *Quaderno* 22 of the Accademia dei Lincei (1976), pp. 113–37. Even Nicolet seems to me to end by accepting too much.

[39] See Weber (1972) 779–81.

[40] However, to the end of the Republic the patrician families were always barred from holding the office of tribune of the plebs: witness the career of the patrician Julius Caesar.

14

to this aristocracy usually came through the election to the consulate of a 'new man', someone whose family had hitherto been outside the select circle. The numbers of these new men were, naturally enough, sufficient to provide the recruits that the old patrician order had been unable to acquire under the ancient rules that were never altered. They were drawn from the substantial body of men of means, normally men with landed wealth, who dominated local politics in the municipalities and regions outside the city of Rome and who provided steady support at the centre for the nobility. The appearance relatively late in the Republic of special interest-groups, notably the *publicani* (tax-farmers and holders of public contracts), sometimes introduced minor complications into the political picture but the notion that they were responsible for the injection of class conflict within the upper classes is a modern fallacy.[41]

In the course of our discussion we shall be considering one or another of these developments when required. Here it will suffice merely to enumerate the main variables among the city-states: size of population and of territory; natural resources, notably grain, metals, timber; degree of urbanization, in the sense of function and interest rather than of residence; the economic infrastructure of slaves and free non-citizens; scale and sources of wealth. However, all the city-states had in common one feature, the incorporation of peasants, craftsmen and shopkeepers into the political community as members, as citizens; even those who had neither the obligation nor the privilege of bearing arms, it is important to underscore. They were not at first (and in some communities never) members with full rights, not citizens in the full sense that the term acquired in classical Greece and Rome. But even limited recognition was without precedent in history; it is symbolized by the very inventive political subdivision of the state into smaller territorial units, 'demes' in Athens and other Greek *poleis*, 'tribes' in Rome, most of which were rural.[42] Any account of Greek or Roman politics must properly acknowledge that radical socio-political innovation.

One further variable requires consideration: a few states acquired

---

[41] See, e.g., C. Nicolet, *L'ordre équestre à l'époque républicaine* 1 (Bibliothèque des Ecoles françaises d'Athènes et de Rome 207, 1966), pp. 255–69.

[42] See Weber (1972) 800–1. Despite the obvious etymology, the Latin *tribus*, which lacked a kinship element, had nothing in common with the English 'tribe' in the anthropological sense; see ch. 2 below at nn. 42, 49.

control over relatively extensive foreign territory, either incorporating it completely, or dominating and exploiting it without formally (or even substantively) destroying all independence, or varying the extent and nature of the control from place to place. From the available information analysis is possible in only three cases – Sparta, Athens and Rome – but there is reason to think that this critical variable was absent elsewhere (save perhaps for Rhodes and in a patchy way for Thebes and Thessaly). And in each of these three the economic, social and political effects were radically different.

The Dark-Age origins and growth of the Spartan system in Laconia are irrecoverable. Then, before 700 B.C., Sparta made the decisive move of conquering Messenia and reducing its population to helotage. That led to the conversion of the Spartan citizenry into a closed class of full-time soldiers supported by the compulsory labour of helots, a process that was completed by about 600 B.C. following the suppression of a large-scale and tenacious Messenian revolt. The system had its flaws and anomalies – the survival of an aristocracy within the Spartiate élite and the emergence of such curious statuses as the so-called Inferiors, the *mothakes* and the *neodamodeis* – but they need not detain us.

The early history of Athens is in important respects no less mysterious. We do not know, for example, how and when the whole of Attica (about 2,500 km²) was incorporated into a single *polis*, in which there was no status distinction between the people of Athens on the one hand and the members of Marathon, Eleusis and the other villages and communities within Attica. No other Greek city-state had a comparably large territorial and demographic base (barring the different, conquest-based territory of Sparta). Nor did any other, apart from the small island of Siphnos in the Cyclades, have the inestimable advantage of substantial silver mines within its own confines (at Laureion in the south-eastern region of Attica). The ancient authorities were agreed that the mines were the key to the naval expansion that gave Athens a decisive role in the Persian wars,[43] and the impetus to establish a maritime empire immediately thereafter. Some expansionist moves had been made earlier, under the Pisistratid tyranny when quasi-military settlements were found-

[43] The sources are laid out by J. Labarbe, *La loi navale de Thémistocle* (Bibl. de la Fac. de Philos. et Lettres de l'Univ. de Liège 143, 1957), pp. 10–17, and discussed at excruciating length in ch. 1.

ed in the Dardanelles region, but it was the fifth-century empire that justifies the inclusion of Athens among the conquest-states. Not much territory was acquired in the strict sense, apart from the enclaves confiscated from subject-states for settlement by Athenians, and the subjects retained considerable independence. Nevertheless, the empire more than doubled Athenian public revenues, enabling the state to carry out a large programme of naval construction and other public works, paid for in large part by imperial income and otherwise by the richer citizens; and to provide at least partial employment for many poorer citizens, chiefly through the navy.

The Roman development was increasingly of a different order both qualitatively and quantitatively. From the outset the Roman Republic fully incorporated some neighbouring communities whenever that was possible: that meant including their territories in the *ager Romanus* and their citizenry in the Roman citizen-body (though as time went on with subtle differentiations with respect to their rights). By the time Rome had conquered the whole of Italy south of the Po River, that is, by the early third century B.C., the Roman citizen-body therefore greatly outnumbered the Athenian at its peak, and the latter was much the largest of any Greek city-state. And Rome did not stop, though it already possessed the greatest land-empire seen hitherto in the city-state world. In the final three hundred years of the Republic there were probably not a dozen when a Roman army was not engaged abroad. For the last two centuries, it has been estimated that the median of adult male citizens involved in any year was 13 per cent, rising as high as 35 per cent in some years.[44] These are approximations, to be sure, but no reasonable margin of error one wishes to allow will weaken the implication of these staggering numbers, probably without parallel in history.

Fundamental changes in the society were the inevitable consequence. Landowning at the top end of the scale reached acreages undreamed of before, resting on a slave labour force again without precedent. Continued block grants of citizenship to Latins, Italian 'allies' and some other groups, and the almost automatic grant of citizenship to the freed slaves of citizens swelled the total of 'Romans' far beyond what had already been a figure incompatible

---

[44] Harris (1979) 9–10, 256–7; Hopkins (1978) 31–5. The detailed analysis of Brunt (1971b) is fundamental for the period 225 B.C. to A.D. 14.

with the Aristotelian ideal of a city-state (and with the actual functioning of city-state institutions).[45] Freed slaves had only restricted rights in the first generation; of the others, an increasingly large proportion resided at distances from Rome that severely impeded direct political participation for all but the rich and their retainers. At the same time, a substantial sector of the peasantry were compelled to abandon their holdings by a process more complex than is often appreciated. There was a steady migration to the cities, above all to the city of Rome. Calculations of the population of Rome are not much better than guesses, but there is one indicator that has the appearance of accuracy: the list of the citizens in the city of Rome (and only in the city of Rome) eligible to receive free grain numbered 320,000 when Caesar became dictator (Suetonius, *Caesar* 41.5).

All this military activity represented power, in its narrow sense of force, exercised abroad. Our concern, however, is primarily with the internal functioning of the state. What power did it have to enforce its decisions in the many fields of behaviour for which it laid down rules? The ancient city-state had no police other than a relatively small number of publicly owned slaves at the disposal of the different magistrates, from archons and consuls down to market inspectors,[46] and in Rome the lictors, normally lower-class citizens, in attendance on the higher magistrates. That is hardly surprising: the organized police force is a nineteenth-century creation. But – and this is crucial and exceptional – the army was not available for large-scale police duties until the city-state was replaced by a monarchy. The contrast on this score with the Italian city-states of the late Middle Ages is noteworthy.[47] The ancient city-state army

---

[45] I oversimplify; see Gauthier (1974), with bibliography, and the discussion of citizenship below in ch. 4.

[46] The evidence for public slaves is sporadic; for Athens, see O. Jacob, *Les esclaves publics à Athènes* (Bibl. de la Fac. de Philos. et Lettres de l'Univ. de Liège 35, 1928; repr., New York 1979); for Rome, W. Eder, *Servitus publica* (Wiesbaden 1980), Mommsen (1899) bk II ch. 12.

[47] In this context the familiar ideological discussion by humanists, notably Machiavelli, of the relative merits or demerits of mercenaries and citizen militia is irrelevant. See C. C. Bayley, *War and Society in Renaissance Florence* (Toronto 1961), who, on the rare occasions when he remembers that there were problems of internal order, takes it for granted that both mercenaries and militia were always available to suppress civic unrest; cf. W. M. Bowsky, 'The Medieval Commune and Internal Violence: Police Power and Public Safety in Siena, 1287–1355', *American Historical Review* 73 (1967) 2–17.

was a citizen militia, in existence as an army only when called up for action against the external world. What Nicolet has said of Rome was equally true of the Greek *polis*: 'At any given time when the state was at peace with its neighbours Rome had no army at all.'[48] It was, furthermore, a socially select militia: in principle, both cavalry and infantry were required to equip themselves, and that automatically reduced the poorer 'half' of the citizenry to marginal service, in the fleet or the light-armed auxiliaries, or to complete exemption save in emergencies.

One can easily list exceptions to the ideal type of the ancient citizen army just presented. Sparta was always an exception. Some states had small, élite standing armies, such as the 'Sacred Band' of 300 in Thebes. The Athenian navy (and perhaps a few others) offered poor citizens an opportunity to serve as paid rowers. In the fourth century B.C., the Greek cities increasingly employed mercenary soldiers in their wars; that was an important symptom of a changing social and political situation, but neither the mercenaries nor their professional commanders played a role in internal politics (unless tyrants were in control).[49] The scale of the Roman effort forced repeated reductions in the minimum financial qualification for service and the payment of a subsistence allowance to soldiers on duty. By the end of the second century B.C., indeed, the very notion of a self-equipped militia was abandoned; that is one reason, as we shall see, why the final century of the Roman Republic presents at best a distorted version of city-state politics.

None of this falsifies the general formulation about the city-state and its armies,[50] but one important distinction between Greece and Rome imposes a qualification. The strictness of Roman military discipline is a commonplace (notably Polybius 6.37–8); on-the-spot penalties included the death sentence by order of a commander (and even decimation, the execution of every tenth soldier in a detachment). Greek army discipline seems to have been much more lax, cases of serious punishment without court proceedings rare.[51]

---

[48] Nicolet (1976) 134.
[49] On the relations between the Greek cities and the mercenary commanders and armies they employed, see now Pritchett (1971–9) II ch. 2–4.
[50] See Nicolet (1976) 125–6. His chapters 3–4 present the best balanced account (with bibliography) of those aspects of Roman army history that are relevant to the present discussion.
[51] On Rome, see, e.g., G. R. Watson, *The Roman Soldier* (London 1969), pp. 117–26; on Greece, Pritchett (1971–9) II ch. 12.

Closely linked with that difference was the Roman concept of a magistrate's *imperium* (to be examined in the third chapter), which allowed him, if he were high enough in the hierarchy of offices, to exercise *coercitio* in everyday civilian life against a citizen (and of course against women and non-citizens) who failed to obey an order; that could mean a fine, confiscation of a piece of property, imprisonment, possibly banishment, but not capital punishment, without any process of law or any right of appeal. *Imperium* was an undefined power; it embraced anything within a magistrate's sphere of competence that had not been excluded by law. Hence, as Mommsen observed, a magistrate's *coercitio*, if within the acknowledged (and wide) limits, 'might be unjust (*unbillig*), it could never be illegal (*rechtswidrig*)'.[52] His Greek counterpart could, for example, fine a delinquent shopkeeper, but he could not exercise *coercitio* in this or any other situation unless specifically authorized to do so by a legislative act, and no such act ever allowed him to imprison or banish.

Against individuals the Romans thus had a small and rudimentary police machinery, mostly in the area of criminal law. When large numbers of more or less organized individuals were involved, however, the machinery could not possibly have coped. What then? The available evidence, both Greek and Roman, is too skimpy to provide a clear answer but it is sufficiently suggestive. In 186 B.C. the Roman élite took fright at the widespread adoption of Bacchic rites in Rome and much of Italy, especially in the lower classes. Our one narrative source, a dozen pages in Livy (39.8–19) nearly two centuries after the event, wholly partisan, melodramatic and in places fictitious, insists on a mass conspiracy that was successfully suppressed. Some historians have concluded that this affair shows 'efficient police organization in a crisis',[53] but that is not how I read Livy's account. The assistants normally at the disposal of the magistrates were supported by their personal slaves and dependants and by specially appointed guards and night-watchmen, but they alone could not have questioned, imprisoned and finally executed thousands. Nor does Livy say that they acted alone: he reports widespread denunciation of individuals and 'police' action by

[52] Mommsen (1899) 39 (bk 1 ch. 4 is devoted to *coercitio*); cf. Mommsen (1887–8) 1 134–61. The palliatives provided by tribunician intervention or by the institution of *provocatio* need not concern us.
[53] Lintott (1968) 106.

ordinary citizens who *volunteered* in response to the consul's appeal in a *contio*, an informal public meeting.[54] The language of that appeal as formulated by Livy (39.16.13) is vague: do your duty 'wherever you may be stationed, whatever you may be ordered'. That is not how a Roman army was levied: a *dilectus* – the technical word for call-up perfectly familiar to Livy – had to be voted by the Senate and then conducted by a consul according to recognized procedures. The word *dilectus*, the requisite senatorial decision and the consular procedure are all missing from the narrative. Nor are they visible in Appian's account of the destruction of Gaius Gracchus, when, the historian writes, the consul had 'armed men' at his disposal (*Civil War* 1.113, 116).

An Athenian parallel offers further illumination. In 415 B.C. there occurred a double sacrilege, the mutilation of the herms and the 'profanation' of the Eleusinian mysteries; coinciding with the outset of the expedition against Sicily, they brought about a near-panic. As in Rome in 186 and 121, all the organs of government were involved in the investigation and punishments, and ordinary citizens were mobilized to denounce and to police. This time the textual evidence is specific: the Council, Andocides reports (1.45), asked the *strategoi* to summon citizens living in the city to assemble under arms at a number of designated places.[55]

The two incidents had significantly different political overtones: the Roman Senate saw in the Bacchanalians a subversive threat from below, whereas in Athens in 415 the fear was of a conspiracy aimed at both the Sicilian expedition and democratic institutions (whether or not either fear was well founded is beside the point).[56] What they had in common was the fact that a large proportion of the citizens possessed military arms as a matter of obligation and were practised in their use. Such a military system was without precedent (and with scarcely any later examples), and created a unique relationship between the armed forces and both their commanders and the

---

[54] A *contio* was a mass meeting addressed by one or more magistrates or senators which dissolved without taking formal action. On the fundamental distinction between a *contio* and an assembly, see Taylor (1966) ch. 2.

[55] Andocides is notoriously unreliable but this item is confirmed by a sentence in Thucydides (6.61.2) reporting that armed citizens slept in the Theseum, one of the stations mentioned by Andocides.

[56] Paradoxically, the Athenian affair is much more fully documented than the Roman and also more obscure. The best account remains that of J. Hatzfeld, *Alcibiade* (Paris 1951), pp. 158–205.

state.[57] In an internal crisis, or what was held to be a crisis, the army as such was not available as a coercive force, but armed men could be summoned as volunteers. An ancient scholar, paraphrasing a passage in Sallust's lost *Histories*, explained that such volunteers were not soldiers but substitutes for soldiers (*non sunt milites sed pro milite*).[58] The distinction is not merely verbal; it is a fundamental one in political thinking and political psychology. No one could have been commanded to volunteer; the response was not predictable either in numbers or in rapidity; the volunteers were not subject to military discipline nor did they swear the oath of loyalty to his general required of a Roman soldier each time he was called up.[59] On the other hand, in such situations volunteers have always been more 'reliable' than conscripts.

Citizens with ready access to arms were chiefly men who had already served in the militia. It is then tempting to draw conclusions from the undeniably timocratic character of the citizen-army, but matters were not always so simple, as the Athenian experience in 415 indicates.[60] In a situation of outright civil war, when more or less organized armies, both 'official' and 'unofficial', are present *de facto*, the class character of the army might of course become the decisive factor, but civil war marks the failure of political solutions and requires our attention only when we come to that. We shall see

---

[57] Max Weber of course made the point, briefly but sharply: Weber (1972) 756–7; cf. S. Andreski, *Military Organization and Society* (2 ed., London 1968), pp. 34–5, 98–9. Its implications, or at least the consequential nuances, seem to me to be overlooked in the debate initiated by A. M. Snodgrass, 'The Hoplite Reform and History', *Journal of Hellenic Studies* 85 (1965) 110–22; see most recently P. Cartledge and J. Salmon, *ibid.* 97 (1977) 11–27 and 84–101; Spahn (1977) 70–83.

[58] Servius, *Commentary on Virgil's Aeneid* 2.157; cf. Isidore of Seville, *Etym.* 9.3.54. The summons was called an *evocatio*, not a *dilectus*.

[59] On the oath, see below, ch. 6 at n. 24. Another kind of emergency measure was the declaration by the Senate of a *tumultus*, requiring an immediate mobilization of an army to combat an enemy at the gates, whose presence did not permit the luxury of a proper *dilectus*. The evidence is confused, largely because the common meaning of *tumultus* was an uproar of any kind. When Livy used the word in connection with the Bacchanalian affair (39.16.13), for instance, I believe that he meant it in that general sense, not in its special technical sense. My reason is that the procedures adopted, on his own account, were not those of a 'formal' *tumultus*. If that is right, it then appears that the extension of the declaration of *tumultus* from a foreign enemy to the enemy within did not occur before the first century B.C.

[60] There appears to be an analogous case in the account by Aeneas Tacticus 11.7–10 of the suppression of an aristocratic coup in Argos early in the fourth century B.C.

at the end of chapter 5 that the whole of the last century of the Roman Republic has to be treated as a civil war phase.[61]

[61] The corollary is that all writing from this period about the Roman past is severely distorted by contemporary concerns and judgments, and is not primary source-material except when one can be confident that it truly reflects earlier writing. That is a pity but not an excuse for the common practice of pretending (or hoping) that the best we have is good enough. One need only observe how much of Nicolet (1976), an illuminating book, is really about 'le métier du citoyen' during the civil-war period.

2

AUTHORITY AND PATRONAGE

Neither police action against individual miscreants nor crisis measures against large-scale 'subversion' tells us how a Greek city-state or Rome was normally able to enforce governmental decisions through the whole gamut from foreign policy to taxation and civil law, when they evidently lacked the means with which, in Laski's vigorous language, 'to coerce the opponents of the government, to break their wills, to compel them to submission'.[1] And we are considering states that were politically stable for centuries. Not all were, to be sure, but the critical fact is that the three we have to concentrate on because of the evidence, Athens, Sparta and Rome, were characterized by a continuous acceptance of their political institutions and of the men and classes who operated them. There were many political changes within our time-limits, many sharp political conflicts, many dissatisfied and disgruntled citizens, but the states remained politically stable. For Athens it is enough to recall the rapid reestablishment of the system after the shattering defeat in the Peloponnesian War and the two brief oligarchic coups that the war engendered; for Rome, sufficient proof is provided by the continued willingness of its citizens to serve *en masse* during centuries of unceasing warfare.

The unavoidable conclusion is that, at least in the stable states, acceptance of the institutions and of the system as a whole was existential: their legitimacy rested on their continual and successful existence.[2] That is hardly surprising and even commonplace: the same can be said of many states in the past and the present, though of few (and perhaps none) with so little coercive power readily to hand. In antiquity, only the serious theorists advanced beyond that in their justification of the city-state as the only acceptable political organism. In the *Politics* Aristotle defined man as a *zoön politikon* (1252b9–53a39), and what that meant is comprehensible only in the

[1] Laski (1935) 26–7.
[2] Several such points, stated briefly in the opening pages of the present chapter, will be considered more fully in ch. 6.

light of his metaphysics; hence correct translation requires a cumbersome paraphrase – man is a being whose highest goal, whose *telos* (end), is by nature to live in a *polis*. I suppose most Greeks might have agreed, had they heard of Aristotle and grasped what he was saying, which few did.

Much the more familiar approach was to argue from the past, historical or fictitious, and that is, of course, another socio-political commonplace.[3] Our concern is less with arguments of the 'good-old-days' variety than with the psychological need for identity through a feeling of continuity, and with its concomitant feeling that the basic structure of social existence and the value-system inherited from the past are fundamentally the only right ones for that society. I use the word 'feeling' to signal the unreflective, habitual character of the response: appeals to the *patrios politeia* (ancestral constitution) in Athens or the *res publica* in Rome stirred up a warm emotional glow of rightness, not an analytical or historical inquiry into the precise sense or validity of employment of the terms in the particular context. Thus, in the course of the late fifth-century conflicts in Athens both oligarchs and democrats claimed to be reestablishing the ancestral constitution; four hundred years later, Augustus baldly asserted that in 28–27 B.C. 'I transferred the *res publica* from my power (*potestas*) to the dominion (*arbitrium*) of the Senate and people of Rome' (*Res gestae* 34.1).

That such claims were false more often than not is easily demonstrated, but that is not a very interesting exercise. The pertinent question is not: Did Augustus restore the *res publica*? but: Did Romans and Italians in sufficient numbers persuade themselves that he had? What mattered was the ability of the stable societies to maintain without petrification their strong sense of continuity through change, their resolute acceptance of what the Greeks called *nomos* and the Romans *mos*, habitual practice, usage, custom. In 92 B.C. the Roman censors closed the schools of 'Latin rhetoric' as an undesirable departure from the *mos maiorum*. 'Our ancestors', they are quoted as having decreed, 'laid down what they wished their children to learn and what schools they were to attend. These innovations, which run counter to the tradition and customs of our ancestors, neither please us nor seem right.'[4] Two generations later,

---

[3] I have examined this comparatively in Finley (1975) ch. 2: 'The Ancestral Constitution'.

[4] Suetonius, *De grammaticis et rhetoribus* 25.1.

just such private schools of rhetoric were flourishing in Rome, drawing their pupils from the young of the upper classes.

Such contradictory claims and attitudes 'are inherent in any situation in which the past is arbiter: the past offered examples of either change or no-change as one wished. There is no more striking situation than the long process by which the Roman state formally introduced a host of foreign divinities into the official cult, though nothing might appear to be a more blatant departure from the *mos maiorum*.[5] Yet Cicero could overlook the whole process, of which he had considerable knowledge, and attribute Rome's greatness to divine favour in return for strict observance of the rites and cults established by Romulus and King Numa (*On the Nature of the Gods* 3.5). I do not pretend to grasp his mental processes, nor that of the Greeks and Romans generally on this subject. The calendar was crowded with sacred days and festivals, each with its strict rituals meticulously observed, not infrequently with consequent delay and even disruption of both public and private business. No public action and few private ones were undertaken without supplicating the gods beforehand through prayers and sacrifices, and without repaying them for success afterwards with gifts and dedications. Often enough, among the Romans always, the gods were also consulted beforehand in ritually specified ways about the prospects of success in public matters. Roman religiosity moved Greek observers to awed comment,[6] notably in comparative contexts as against the Carthaginians and other peoples they had overcome.

Proof of the rightness of the ritual procedures was a simple pragmatic one: success demonstrated that Zeus or Jupiter (or whoever) had been favourably disposed. In early times, before the creation of a centralized city-state, the main beneficiaries were the aristocratic families who controlled local cult-centres. With the emergence of the state and state cults, religion was a factor in providing legitimacy to the system as a whole: the psychological effect of a continuous, massive, solemn sharing in state rites that passed the pragmatic test over long periods. There is neither documentary evidence, however, nor reason to think that policy-

[5] See J. A. North, 'Conservatism and Change in Roman Religion', *Papers of the British School at Rome* 44 (1976) 1–12.
[6] The classic text is Polybius 6.56.6. A good introduction to the subject is provided by Kroll (1933) II ch. 5.

making was ever determined or deflected by reference to divine will or divine precept. As we shall see in chapter 4, the conduct of a battle or a war was occasionally disrupted by a festival or an unfavourable omen; the Roman élite manipulated the rites of consultation in order to delay action; but that appears to have been the sum of it. No doctrinal or, in a proper sense, ethical justification was provided by religion for either the structure of the system or the governmental policies being pursued or proposed. Therefore, although I do not underestimate the impact of religion, I do not find it the decisive, let alone a sufficient, factor in the process by which such great authority was acquired by the system and then maintained for a long time. That process was multifarious and it varied considerably from community to community. A proper inquiry into the subject would be nothing less than a history of the material relations both between the state and its citizens and among the citizens or classes of citizens, a history of war, 'national' pride and patriotism, and a history of ideology in all its senses, including both consciously and unconsciously held ideas, beliefs, cultural norms, values. Such an inquiry obviously cannot be undertaken here, but a few specific themes need to be considered for future reference.

The first is fundamental to all the others. Because no city-state was genuinely egalitarian and many were not democratic either, political stability rested on the acceptance in all classes of the legitimacy of status and status-inequality in some measure, not only of the existence of *boni* but also of their right to greater wealth, greater social standing and political authority. Only the limits, the qualifications, the nuances varied. The point is not that Plato or Aristotle, Polybius or Cicero thought so but that the *improbi* and *hoi polloi* thought so, too, or at least behaved as if they did. Some outright Greek oligarchies were stable, most obviously Corinth. Even in Athens under what modern historians tend to call the 'radical democracy', the *demos* never produced spokesmen in the Assembly from their own ranks. In Rome, the magistrates, who were always restricted to a small circle of the wealthiest families, rigidly controlled and limited the power of the assemblies, in which the voting procedure was anyway heavily weighted against the lower classes.[7]

Hierarchical values were built into the education of Greeks and

---

[7] The evidence about the procedure in the tribal assembly and the *concilium plebis* is surprisingly unsatisfactory but my reading of it leads to the statement in the text.

Romans of all classes – education in the broad sense that Durkheim distinguished from pedagogy,[8] a process for which the nearest English equivalent is 'upbringing'. It is a truism that both education and pedagogy always have the primary function of transmitting to successive generations the prevailing values of the given society. The role of the state is almost irrelevant: in the ancient world, apart from the inevitable exception of Sparta, the state played little direct part in education and none at all in pedagogy – a critical flaw in Plato's eyes – barring a few relatively late interventions in higher education, as in the schools of law and the endowed chairs of rhetoric or philosophy under the Roman Empire, or the occasional expulsion of undesirable teachers or schools. Higher education, that is, any pedagogy above the most elementary reading, writing and counting, was of course restricted to a small élite, though popular antagonism was notoriously aroused from time to time – always by other members of the élite – because of a threat, alleged or real, to prevailing values and institutions. Aristophanes' *Clouds* is the paradigmatic document, the expulsion of the heads of three Greek philosophical schools from Rome in 155 B.C. the model incident. It is not to be imagined that ordinary Athenian citizens seriously attended to what Socrates and the Sophists were saying, or Romans to Carneades and his colleagues nearly three hundred years later.

Yet these ordinary citizens, those who were illiterate as well as those who were technically literate, were far more educated (in the non-pedagogical sense) than historians usually allow. The communities were relatively (and often absolutely) small 'face-to-face societies',[9] in which there was continuing contact from childhood with public life: hence, given the extension of political rights to peasants, craftsmen and shopkeepers, there was a larger element of political education in the process of growing up than in most other societies before or since. Whether or not one believes, with John Stuart Mill, in the value of such education is not important here.[10] What I am concerned to stress, against the standard neglect (or denial) by historians, is that such a process was inherent in the

[8] E. Durkheim, *Education and Sociology*, trans. S. D. Fox (New York and London 1956).
[9] I take the phrase from Peter Laslett's interesting essay in Laslett (1956) ch. 10. The large city-states remained face-to-face societies because of the way life was lived in villages and individual urban districts. We shall return to this in ch. 4.
[10] See briefly Finley (1973*b*) 30–2.

28

system. 'In a democratic state', Walzer has recently written in a contemporary context,

every citizen has political decisions to make. I don't mean only the decision to vote or not to vote, to support the Democrats or Republicans, to attend this meeting or sign that petition . . . It is a special feature of democratic government that the experiences of leaders are not alien to ordinary citizens. With only a modest imaginative effort, the citizen can put himself in the place of his elected representative. Because he can do that, and commonly does, he engages in what I want to call . . . anticipative and retrospective decision-making . . . Vicarious decision-making precedes and follows actual decision-making.[11]

I believe that to have been more common in the face-to-face city-state than it is in our world, even in the ancient non-democratic communities on an undoubtedly less intense level.

I have insisted on the political education of the illiterate as well as the literate because the ancient world remained predominantly one of the spoken, not the written word.[12] In politics and the law that is evident from the place of speeches in the work of both Greek and Roman historians, from the whole of the argument in Aristotle's *Rhetoric*, or from Cicero's constant boasting of his success in persuading the Senate by a speech to adopt one policy rather than another. Freedom of speech (when it existed) meant literally the freedom to 'speak in public, in the discussions that preceded any collective decision', not the freedom to have unpopular or unacceptable ideas or to discuss them among friends and pupils.[13] As a corollary, the most effective way to eliminate undesirable ideas – and undesirable individuals, political opponents – was by exile or capital punishment. That prevented oral communication, and nothing else mattered significantly.[14]

The implications and consequences of an oral culture with a component of literacy are complex and often inaccessible to us. Direct observation of contemporary pre-literate societies and of those that have crossed the threshold to literacy has not proved

---

[11] M. Walzer, 'Political Decision-Making and Political Education', in *Political Theory and Political Education*, ed. M. Richter (Princeton 1980), pp. 159–76, at p. 159.

[12] I have tried to draw some of the political consequences in Finley (1977), though with a different stress from what follows immediately in the present account.

[13] Lanza (1979) 55, an important study although I do not agree with his view that a significant change set in during the fourth century B.C. in Athens.

[14] This point is developed at some length in Finley (1977).

helpful in the study of ancient politics. The discovery of what Goody, in a pioneering anthropological inquiry into the subject, has called the 'enabling effects' of literacy,[15] tends to bemuse the observer into confusing literacy and mere knowledge of letters: Greece and Rome were 'really literate societies', Goody writes, and 'the ease of alphabetic reading and writing was probably an important consideration in the development of political democracy in Greece'.[16] Yet, whatever one may mean by a 'really literate society', whatever the undeniable importance of literacy in the history of philosophy, science, historiography or 'religion of the book', for politics the accent needs modification. One comparison between Athens (or indeed any Greek *polis*) and Rome is illuminating. In both, the archaic struggle for a written law code was rightly looked back upon as critical in breaking the power-monopoly of the old aristocracy; hence the Greek tradition of the archaic 'lawgiver', best known through the historical Solon and the legendary Lycurgus, and the long accounts (no matter how fictitious in the details) by the Roman annalists of the XII Tables and of the later *ius Flavianum*. But the application and efficacy of all law codes depend on the interpretation by magistrates and courts, and unless the right of interpretation is 'democratized', the mere existence of written laws changes little.

The plain fact is that never in antiquity did any but the élite (or their direct agents) consult documents and books. I do not count such 'documents' as formal receipts, announcements of the name of candidates in local elections, or such signs as 'Beware the dog', any more than I share historians' enthusiasm whenever they find examples of the ability of illiterates to scrawl a signature on a document they could not read.[17] Even in the courts the Greek juries only heard the relevant statutes read out in the course of the proceedings, as they heard verbal testimony, and they then rendered their verdict on the spot, without any discussion among themselves. In classical Athens, and presumably in other Greek democracies, the juries were large, representative of wide strata of the population, and plenipotentiary. That is to say, no class of

[15] Goody (1968) 1.   [16] Goody (1968) 42 and 55, respectively.
[17] On the only documentation we have, see H. C. Youtie, 'Hypographeus: The Social Impact of Illiteracy in Graeco-Roman Egypt', *Zeitschrift für Papyrologie und Epigraphik* 17 (1975) 201–21; 'Agrammatos: An Aspect of Greek Society in Egypt', *Harvard Studies in Classical Philology* 75 (1971) 161–76.

professional jurists ever developed, so that the popular juries both interpreted the law and determined matters of fact, guided solely by the speeches prepared for the parties by more or less professional pleaders and by the quotations within the speeches of laws or decrees.[18] In Rome, in contrast, juristic interpretation became highly professionalized, and the jurists, like the courts, were drawn exclusively from the élite. Popular 'semi-literacy', in sum, made little contribution one way or the other.

To be sure, even in our own world most people rely heavily on a truly literate minority for their information and judgments, often by oral communication. Yet there is a fundamental difference when compared with any society, including the Graeco-Roman, in which there was *no* popular 'literature', *no* mass media, *no* popular pamphlets or broadsheets, *no* popular magazines or novels. An archaic law code would have been rather analogous to the Latin Bible, a venerated document but a closed book. The long resistance of the Church to vernacular translations of the Bible, in the west at least, is therefore a pointer to the realities of ancient literacy. When fundamental documents are accessible only to an élite for study and reflection, the rest of the society is heavily subject to their interpretation – of the law, of the will of the gods, of what is right and wrong, of the rules of behaviour, including right political behaviour. That was the situation in antiquity, and, in my view, it strengthened acceptance of the élite and of its claim to dominate. And the more the interpretation, the rules and the values could be sanctified by *nomos* and *mos maiorum* the better. In this area, the difference between democratic Athens and oligarchic Rome lay primarily not in popular literacy but in the fact that in Athens the élite divided in the critical period, with the dominant section accepting democratic institutions and offering themselves as leaders, an offer that the *demos* did not reject or resist.

What, then, was expected of the leaders; in effect, of the government, the state, whose rightness and legitimacy were generally acknowledged openly or tacitly? There were intangibles to be gained: the feeling of identification with the group, the sense that order, security, freedom, even life itself were made possible by (and only by) the prevailing arrangements and institutions. All that is valuable but man does not live by ideology alone, and a substantial

---

[18] The capital importance of this point has been stressed by Lanza (1979) 59–61.

proportion of the Greek and Roman citizens had a low standard of living that was under perpetual threat. They expected, or at least wished and hoped for, some measure of assistance, even if no more than what has been called 'subsistence crisis insurance'.[19] Hence the material base – or aspects if one dislikes base – of political *auctoritas* requires serious consideration.

Again the differences within the ancient world must bulk large in any detailed examination, and again the conquest-states constituted a group apart. Not only did they provide unparalleled psychological satisfaction but they also secured from their victims substantial material benefits, in land, in money or in compulsory labour, some of which flowed to the lower classes of the citizenry no matter how successful the élites may have been in bringing about a one-sided division of the spoils.[20] Particularly notable, though incalculable, was the value of 'tribute' (in whatever form) in keeping down the internal financial contribution required for the varied public activities incumbent on a city-state, or at least in stimulating a scale of activity that would otherwise have been very burdensome if not unattainable.

In the city-states, including those that did not fall within the conquest category, governmental costs, including the military, fell almost entirely on the wealthier classes of the citizenry in so far as they could not be shifted to external subjects. Direct taxation, whether on property or on the person (a poll-tax), was a mark of tyranny (internal or external) and was rejected by both oligarchies and democracies. Exceptions were made to meet military needs when other sources of public revenue were insufficient. In major crises, such as the Peloponnesian War or the Hannibalic War, these 'extraordinary' levies became frequent and burdensome. Nevertheless, the critical point is that they had to be specifically voted each year when required. They were never converted into a regular tax, and the poor were wholly exempt in the Greek *poleis*, largely so in Rome.[21] In effect, then, the citizen-poor, and in particular the peasantry, were largely free from taxation: occasional sales taxes,

---

[19] Scott (1977) 23.   [20] See Finley (1978a).

[21] On the general pattern see briefly Finley (1973a) 89–96, (1976a) 18–21; in detail, R. Thomsen, *Eisphora* (Copenhagen 1964), C. Nicolet, *Tributum* (Bonn 1976) The *vectigal* levied on the Roman *ager publicus* was not a departure from the basic principle: see Nicolet, pp. 79–86. Nor was the taxation of land owned outside Italy by Roman citizens.

harbour dues and first-fruits to the gods did not add up to a significant burden. That is why taxation, which was so central in late medieval and modern social struggles, hardly ever appears as an issue in classical antiquity before the Roman Empire. Furthermore, as the poor were in the great majority self-employed in the country and in the city, the peasants were also free from the burden of rents. The tenant farmer and the sharecropper were a phenomenon of the Hellenistic world and of imperial Rome (perhaps beginning in the later Republic), not of the city-state.

These 'negative gains' are not to be underestimated, but they cannot be said to have established of themselves a solid material base for political authority. What direct, positive benefits can be discovered? The great wealth accumulated by Roman senators or tax-farmers as a direct consequence of conquest and empire merely helps to explain why they preferred oligarchy. My question is not about them but about the poor, the majority of the citizenry in the city-states, and in chapter 5 we shall consider in some detail how they sought governmental support and how their failure in the long run (though a very long run) eroded the appeal of the traditional institutions. For the present, a few broad, and therefore unqualified, statements will suffice.[22] Land hunger was central, as in every agrarian society, and the list of attempted solutions is a long one, throughout Greece in the archaic period, in fifth-century Athens, continuously in Rome. But notably the solutions were external, through emigration, not internal. They normally entailed removal of the beneficiaries from the political community, *de facto* when not *de iure*, and of course failed to prevent the same demands, the same crises, from recurring in later generations. Chronic anxiety over the grain staple induced a range of measures to secure the necessary imports, to restrain prices and to check profiteering, but it was not until the Hellenistic age that the Greek cities themselves began to buy corn from abroad systematically; not until Sicily became the first Roman province at the end of the third century b.c. that the Roman state itself became actively concerned with the supply for the city of Rome (characteristically, at the expense of her subjects); not until the onset of the civil wars that the Roman corn dole began

---

[22] The basic sources for what follows in this paragraph have been collected by H. Bolkestein, *Wohltätigkeit und Armenpflege im vorchristlichen Altertum* (Utrecht 1939, repr. New York 1979), pp. 248–86, 749–79.

its long history. Financial assistance to invalids, war orphans and widows was minimal and spasmodic, when it existed at all.

Only in Athens, to the best of our knowledge, did the state provide massive economic support for the poor through large-scale employment in the navy and through the provision of pay, in the form of a modest *per diem*, for the whole range of offices, including the thousands of jurymen and even, from the beginning of the fourth century, those who attended meetings of the assembly.[23] No one could have supported a family on state pay alone, not even naval pay in those years when naval activity was most intense. There is nevertheless no warrant for the frequent dismissal of pay for office and other financial benefits as a negligible factor in Athenian government and politics.[24] The buttressing effect was substantial and politically significant; one could reasonably call it a form of permanent, governmental 'subsistence crisis insurance'. Nothing else in classical Athenian institutions so enraged anti-democratic publicists. That dislike underlay the insistent attack on the 'demagogues', as we have already seen in Plato's sneer at pastrycooks in his *Gorgias*.

There is no need to draw any implication about aristocratic or oligarchic hard-heartedness, or about a wish that the poor go under. At least three other elements enter the picture: first, the close link between democracy, lower-class participation in government and pay for office, about which I shall have more to say in subsequent chapters; secondly, the argument that the aim and consequence were impoverishment of the wealthy – the *demos* 'demand payment for singing, running, dancing and sailing on ships in order that they may get the money and the rich become poorer' (Ps.-Xenophon, *Constitution of Athens* 1.13) – a mere debating-trick with which I am not presently concerned; and thirdly, a belief that the élite, if anyone, should provide subsistence crisis insurance. Again there is no question of soft- or hard-heartedness. In antiquity, at any rate, benevolence was rarely disinterested, either towards equals or towards inferiors. One objective was the establishment of a patron-client relationship and nexus of relationships, and, flowing from that, further sanction for the power-and-authority structure pre-

---

[23] See Finley (1978*b*) 114–24.
[24] Among recent writers, Kluwe (1977) 46–55; Meier (1980), esp. 252–3, but with inconsistencies, e.g. 256.

vailing in the particular society. It was a weakness of the oligarchs of his day, Aristotle suggested, that they had abandoned the practice of assigning unpaid public services to the high civic offices, of giving public feasts, and of donating public monuments, all ways of securing popular acquiescence to oligarchic rule (*Politics* 1321a31–42). Such 'ritualized affirmation of inequality', Barrington Moore has noted in an important generalization, is effective only 'as long as in the end it somehow contributes to the social good *as perceived and defined in that society*' (my italics).[25]

The stress in Aristotle, as generally among ancient authors, was on what may be called community patronage, that is, large-scale private expenditure, whether compulsory or voluntary, for communal purposes – temples and other public works, theatre and gladiatorial shows, festivals and feasts – in return for popular approval; often, as we shall see, for popular support in the advancement of political careers.[26] Such outlays had a tradition stretching far back in time, before there was a proper public fisc, though the original concentration was on the locality, the village or deme in which the members of the élite had their base. Then came the classical *polis*, with its formalized institutions, including the provision and control of public finance. Community patronage had to be at least partially integrated into the new institutional framework if it were not to be a disruptive factor. We are unable to

---

[25] B. Moore, Jr, *Injustice: the Social Bases of Obedience and Revolt* (London 1978), pp. 41–2. Eighteenth-century commentators of course had an instant perception of the pattern; see, e.g., Montesquieu's remarks about the Greek city-states, *Esprit des lois*, Bk VII, ch. 3. I make scarcely any reference to the recent outpouring of sociological and anthropological literature on patronage because I have found little of it helpful. The field of study is restricted to an odd combination of small societies in the colonial (or ex-colonial) world, backward agrarian regions in the Mediterranean basin, and machine politics in big American cities. The vast expanse of historical societies is ignored, so that, e.g., A. Weingrod has produced a typology in which the Roman *clientela* cannot be accommodated (though 'patron' and 'client' are of course words coined by the Romans): 'Patrons, Patronage and Political Parties', *Comparative Studies in Society and History* 10 (1963) 376–400, reprinted in Schmidt (1977) 323–37. For a detailed bibliography, see J. C. Scott's appendix in Schmidt (1977) or S. N. Eisenstadt and L. Roniger, 'Patron–Client Relations as a Model of Structuring Social Exchange', *Comparative Studies . . .* 22 (1980) 42–77.

[26] Community patronage reached its crescendo in the Hellenistic and Roman monarchies, and we now have a massive, wide-ranging study: Veyne (1976). My references to Veyne in what follows are restricted to his primarily introductory sections on the city-states, with which my fundamental disagreement will be evident.

trace in detail the steps by which that was accomplished, but the outcome of the process was a sharply varied one, in direct correlation with the degree of popular participation in the new political system, with the extent of democratization in short.[27] We must look closely at the main variations.

The Greek word Aristotle used in his criticism of the oligarchs, which I have rendered as 'public service', is *leitourgia*, conventionally transliterated by ancient historians as 'liturgy', not without considerable semantic confusion because of its modern ecclesiastical connotation. The classical Greek liturgy, known from a number of *poleis* but in detail only from Athens, was a formal, institutionalized device whereby certain public services were assigned on a rota system to individual members of the richer sector of the population, who were directly responsible for both the costs and the performance, bypassing the treasury, so to speak. Liturgies were compulsory and honorific at the same time. The element of honour is underscored by the fact that the chief sphere of liturgical activity was religion (which, it will be remembered, included the athletic and dramatic festivals). In Demosthenes' day there were at least 97 annual liturgical appointments in Athens for the festivals, rising to over 118 in a (quadrennial) Panathenaic year.[28] The other main liturgy in Athens (and in some other cities) was the trierarchy, personal command of a naval vessel for one year. Furthermore, though there was a notional minimum expenditure, there was no maximum: most liturgies involved competitions and therefore the additional honour that derived from being victorious encouraged outlays well above the minimum. One defendant in a lawsuit at the end of the fifth century claimed that in the eight final years of the Peloponnesian War he had spent about nine and a half talents on liturgies, more than three times the legal requirement, more than twenty times the minimum property holding needed for liturgical assignment (Lysias 21.1–5). Even after due allowance for exaggeration – the jury would have been no more able to check his figures than we are – the outlay was enormous.

---

[27] My disagreement with Veyne (1976) pivots on his (not always consistently applied) notion that there was no correlation such as I stress because the lower classes were 'depoliticized' even in Athens.

[28] J. K. Davies, 'Demosthenes on Liturgies: a Note', *Journal of Hellenic Studies* 87 (1967) 33–40.

The boasting is revealing. It was standard practice in both political and forensic speeches to draw attention to one's own liturgical service and to the opponent's dereliction. 'Expending my resources for your enjoyment' was how one fourth-century B.C. orator-politician summed up the liturgical principle in a major address (Aeschines 1.11). Not all members of the 'liturgical class' were politically active, but, with negligible exceptions, all politicians were in the liturgical class. *Their* boasting exemplifies a successful functioning of Moore's 'ritualized affirmation of inequality'; it helped to justify the *demos'* entrustment of political leadership to them as a class, and to gain popular support for individual members of the élite in their competition with each other for influence.[29] That seems to me to warrant the inclusion of this peculiar form of community service under the heading of patronage despite the absence of a man-to-man patron–client relationship. And when the classical liturgy-system lost its political usefulness, it was promptly abolished by Demetrius of Phalerum, installed as 'regent' in Athens in 317 B.C. by the Macedonian conquerors in order to replace the democracy by an oligarchy.[30]

The word 'liturgy' did not disappear in the post-*polis* Greek world. It even retained its honorific form in the more or less autonomous Greek cities that survived. In the Hellenistic monarchies, however, a new type of liturgy became widespread and often oppressive; it was now a compulsory burden, in money or in corvée labour, covering a wide range of activities, no longer restricted to the wealthy, and wholly lacking in any element of honour or political advancement. Imperial Rome took over the Hellenistic practice – *leitourgia* under the bilingual Empire was the synonym for the

---

[29] That there were rich citizens who objected to the expense goes without saying. Aristotle warned democracies (not only in Athens) that liturgies and 'demagogic' confiscation of property could incite oligarchic revolutions (*Politics* 1304b20-05a7, 1309a14-20).

[30] For the details, see Ferguson (1911) 55-8, for whom the only issue was preservation of the property of the wealthy; a more perceptive analysis is that of Gehrke (1978) 171-3. A contrary view to mine of the Greek liturgy, denying any possible democratic-political link, will be found in Veyne (1976), esp. 186-200. His only reference to the abolition of liturgies by Demetrius is relegated to an empty footnote (338n119). One wonders how he would classify (or explain) the important Athenian politician and benefactor Xenocles, whose career was halted under Demetrius and resumed when the democracy was restored; C. Ampolo, 'Un politico "evergete" del IV secolo a.C. . . . .', *Parola del Passato* (1979) 167-78.

Latin *munus*[31] – and steadily extended it almost to the breaking-point.

The Romans did not adopt the classical Greek liturgy-system. The difference between the two structures is beautifully exemplified by the navy. At one level, the Roman navy was manned primarily by 'allies', slaves and freedmen: although poor citizens were no doubt also included in the crews, they were marginal, and in particular there was nothing remotely comparable to reliance on the navy as a means of helping to support poor citizens.[32] At another level, the Roman method of financing the fleet and selecting commanders for the individual vessels had nothing in common with the Greek trierarchy. In 214 B.C., when the Hannibalic War required a large additional outlay for the navy, the consuls, on instructions from the Senate, ordered an extraordinary levy on a principle not unlike that of the Greek *eisphora* in similar military emergencies: each member of the higher census classes was required to provide pay, rations and equipment for one to eight sailors, according to his wealth. 'This was the first time', Livy reports (24.11.9), 'when a Roman navy was manned at the expense of private individuals.' We do not know how often that practice was subsequently repeated, but there is no reason to think that it was anything but rare, and the difference from a liturgy is obvious. The former was an emergency measure employed only when public funds ran out, the latter was the normal, annually recurrent way of getting certain things done for the state in times of peace and quiet as well as under war conditions.

The numerous public religious festivals illuminate the difference still further. Alongside the navy they were the chief occasion for Greek liturgies, whereas in Rome the principle was long maintained that they had to be financed from the treasury. In time, however, public funds proved inadequate, not because the treasury was too empty but because the scale and costs of the festivals, and particularly the main games (featuring chariot and horse races), accelerated

---

[31] In Republican Rome a *munus* was any obligation to perform a service for the state, a municipality or even a private person – military service, tax payments, and so on. Its later identification with the post-classical Greek liturgy is irrelevant in the present discussion.

[32] See J. H. Thiel, *Studies on the History of Roman Sea-Power in Republican Times* (Amsterdam 1946), pp. 11–18, 195–8, whose conclusions withstand the criticisms that have been attempted; so also Brunt (1971*b*) 666–70.

at a staggering pace. That was the beginning, from the middle or late third century B.C., of the circus component of 'bread and circuses'. Again the financial burden was not met liturgically; instead, the custom arose whereby the aediles, and for some purposes the praetors, were personally responsible for the burgeoning costs. There was no formal obligation on them, and though the force of public opinion and of their own ambitions for the highest magistracy, the consulship, was as powerful as any threat of legal compulsion, the essential distinction from a liturgy remains. Since, furthermore, the aedileship and praetorship were normally not renewable offices, a small number of men were charged with this burden only once or twice in a lifetime. However, there were other 'circuses' that enabled a larger sector of the élite to offer community patronage. It is sufficient to mention the gladiatorial games, which were private funeral celebrations down to 105 B.C., beginning with one involving three duels in 264 B.C. and rising to a spectacle of thirty pairs of contests extending over three days in about 145 B.C. Veyne is therefore right, in broad terms, when he draws the contrast between a *polis* (Athens) that 'honours the gods by amusing itself' and one (Rome) in which a member of the élite, whether in or out of office, 'gives' the festival to the people.[33] It is a contrast in the way in which the old, archaic form of community patronage was integrated into the new city-state structure, and I believe that it clearly reflects the contrast in the extent and nature of public participation in politics, the contrast between democracy and oligarchy (with a popular component). The Roman élite discovered for themselves the virtue in the advice that Aristotle had given to his contemporary oligarchs.

The ancient sources provide considerable, though not systematic, documentation of the various kinds of community patronage. On the other hand, they are almost completely silent about patronage of individuals outside the élite strata (on which Cicero's *Letters* constitute a massive case-book). That is no excuse for following their lead in a consideration of politics: their silence is a necessary consequence of their specific concerns and is not a sign that private patronage was unimportant.[34] A notorious passage in Aristotle's *Constitution of Athens* (27.3) is a clear pointer. Reporting on

---

[33] Veyne (1976) 396–9.
[34] We shall have more than one occasion in subsequent chapters to note and try to overcome this gap in the available evidence.

Pericles' introduction of a *per diem* allowance to jurors, Aristotle writes: Pericles took this step in order to

> practise counter-demagogy to the wealth of Cimon. For Cimon, who had a princely fortune, not only performed the public liturgies munificently but also fed many of his fellow-demesmen: any member of his deme could come to him daily and receive adequate supplies (*ta metria*); furthermore, none of his estates was fenced in, so that anyone who wished could help himself to the fruit. Now Pericles' property was insufficient for such expenditure and he took the advice of Damonides . . . to distribute to the common people (*hoi polloi*) what belonged to them, and so he introduced a *per diem* to jurors.

Aristotle proceeds to report (but not endorse) the view that Pericles thereby took the first step in the corruption of Athenian government and society. This familiar anti-democratic view requires no further discussion here, but there is also present a profound insight into the political sociology of the *polis*, even though we may discount the crude Pericles-versus-Cimon formula.[35] Why, we must ask, should either have bothered with men so poor that they needed to be given their daily food or a two-obol *per diem* when serving on a jury? The answer has two parts: first, a share in political decision-making, whether directly in the Assembly or indirectly in supporting one leader against another, had been given to the entire citizenry, including the poor; secondly, a large sector of the citizenry always lived on the margin of a subsistence level, in constant danger of falling below. The latter condition had not been changed by the long series of measures that began with Solon and culminated in the fifth-century democracy. The peasant (in Athens and other *poleis*, though not all) was no longer threatened with debt bondage, but that was a negative benefit. Where could he turn for succour in times of bad harvests or other disasters? Either to a more prosperous local landowner or to the state. In other words – and that is what Aristotle was in effect saying – he could become the client of a Cimon or the client of the state.[36]

I will be told that I may not say 'client' because there was nothing

---

[35] I blush to recall that I myself once dismissed this as merely a 'silly explanation': Finley (1962) 19. Over-concentrating on the 'explanation' given for jury pay, I overlooked the larger issue now under examination.

[36] I owe this formulation to an intervention by John Dunn during the discussions in Belfast.

in the Athenian situation, or the Greek generally, that was remotely comparable to the *clientela* of the Roman Republic.[37] Such an objection should be dismissed out of hand. The relationship between patron and client is a reciprocal one between unequals, involving not only a subjective element, the 'evaluation of the relationship' by the client, but also the objective one of a genuine exchange of goods or services.[38] It is also very flexible, not only within any society and even within an individual relationship but also among different societies and epochs. To insist on restricting the terminology (and therefore the institution) to the peculiar Roman type is as unwarranted and stultifying as the reverse, to which I have already taken exception, of so narrowing the definition as to exclude the Roman pattern.[39] Anthropologists and sociologists study either small agrarian communities, in which the typical client is a sharecropper or a landless labourer, or patron–client relations in big-city machine politics. The city-state world lacked the latter and its agrarian poor had a large, usually major component of peasants who owned the plots on which they struggled to survive. That world also had a rare complicating element, slave labour, which created a rural (and urban) labour market qualitatively different from the kind prevailing in present-day Mediterranean or South Asian communities. In consequence, the exchange was not so obvious or straightforward in antiquity, though I do not underestimate the employment by the richer proprietors of free peasants as supplementary seasonal labour, notably at harvest times, and the simple reciprocity that such an exchange represented.[40] Of itself, however, this practice could

---

[37] This argument has recently been made emphatically by H. Strasburger, *Zum antiken Gesellschaftsideal* (Abh. d. Heidelberger Akad. d. Wiss., Philosophisch-historische Klasse 4, 1976), pp. 111–16, followed, e.g., by Schuller (1979) 440 with slight hesitation.

[38] See Scott (1977) 22–5.

[39] See n. 25 above. I take this opportunity to express scepticism of the prevailing view of the Roman Republican *clientela*, in which I find an excess of formalism and of what I can only call mysticism (centring on *fides*); see Brunt (forthcoming), with whom I agree fundamentally. What I am discussing is not illuminated in the extensive scholarly literature cited by Brunt. Throughout I shall employ the words 'patron' and 'client' in their widely recognized sociological sense, not in the technical sense (whatever that may be thought to have been).

[40] The indispensability of seasonal labour to a landowner, especially when slaves constituted the permanent labour force, has been well stressed by P. Garnsey and J. E. Skydsgaard, in *Non-slave Labour in Graeco-Roman Antiquity* (*Proceedings of the Cambridge Philological Soc.*, Supp. 6, 1980), ed. Garnsey.

scarcely lay the foundation for widespread clientage in the country-side, and certainly not in the towns. It cannot answer the question I have posed about the interest of Cimon and Pericles in the free poor.

In the end the answer must be speculative, given the scarcity of evidence. Let us look quickly at three constitutionally different instances:

1. The overthrow of the Pisistratid tyranny in Athens in 510 B.C. was followed by a sharp struggle between aristocratic factions, won by Cleisthenes after he had 'brought the *demos* into his faction'.[41] He proceeded to restructure the governmental machinery, basing it on the more than one hundred demes (parishes) of Attica which he combined into ten new, artificial units called *phylai* (conventionally and misleadingly translated 'tribes') in such a way that each tribe included demes from three different regions within the territory.[42] The purpose of this particular manoeuvre, according to Aristotle, who is our only source to offer a rational (though elliptical and probably inadequate) explanation, was to 'mix everyone up in order to dissolve the previous associations' and thereby 'to give more people a share in public affairs (*politeia*)'.[43]

2. In 386 B.C. Sparta defeated (democratic) Mantinea in Arcadia, ordered the city proper to be dismantled and the inhabitants who resided there to return to their original villages. 'When the pro-prietors found themselves living nearer their estates outside the villages', Xenophon (*Hellenica* 5.2.7) reports, 'experiencing an aristocracy and being rid of the burdensome demagogues, they were pleased with the state of affairs.'[44]

---

[41] Herodotus 5.66; cf. Aristotle, *Constitution of Athens* 20–1.

[42] I shall not continue to write 'tribe' in inverted commas but perhaps I should repeat that these *phylai* had nothing in common with what we call 'tribal society' (any more than did the Roman *tribus*). It is not my intention to discuss the Cleisthenic reform in any detail; the literary evidence is fully laid out in Hignett (1952) ch. 6, though the analysis is unsatisfactory.

[43] The quotation comes from *Politics* 1319b25–7 and *Constitution of Athens* 21.2, respectively. The Greek word *synetheiai*, which I have translated as 'associations', is not easily pinned down. Barker reads 'loyalties', perhaps not an improper extension of the usual sense but one that is not well attested.

[44] The 'demagogues', it should be explained, had been exiled. Unless Xenophon's account is incurably distorted, by 'aristocracy' he did not mean oligarchy, for fifteen years later the city was rebuilt by decision of the popular assembly. See generally S. and H. Hodkinson, 'Mantinea and the Mantinike: Settlement and Society in a Greek Polis', *Annual of the British School at Athens* 76 (1981) 239–96, esp. pp. 261–5, 286–7, 290–1.

3. In Rome, a series of laws passed between 139 and 106 B.C. introduced the secret written ballot into the procedure of the *comitia* and of some courts.[45] This practice was disliked by the élite. Cicero explains why in a 'conversation' with his brother Quintus and Atticus (*Laws* 3.33–9): the secret ballot has 'destroyed the *auctoritas* of the optimates'. But he did not recommend a return to open voting; instead, following a suggestion of Plato's (*Laws* 6.753B–D), he proposed the retention of written ballots as a 'guarantee of popular liberty', but only on condition that they be 'offered and shown willingly to any optimate or person of weight'. In that way, Cicero concludes, 'the appearance of liberty will be granted, the *auctoritas* of the *boni* retained'.

Disparate as these three instances are, they raise one question in common: what was the power exercised by the few over the many individually, which Cleisthenes tried to break in Athens, the Spartans to strengthen in Mantinea, Cicero to restore in Rome by his voting proposal? What were the sanctions they could impose on anyone who broke ranks, who failed to provide the political support expected of him? In 167 B.C., when voting was still open, the Senate proposed a triumph for Aemilius Paulus, but his own soldiers lobbied the tribal assembly against it because of his severe discipline and the meagre share of booty that they had received. A distinguished senator, Marcus Servilius, made an impassioned and successful speech in favour of the proposal, which he is said to have concluded in these words: When we proceed to the vote, 'I shall follow along with them all and I shall learn who are the wicked, the ungrateful, and those who would rather be pandered to ("demagoguized") in war than commanded.'[46] What sort of threat was this? Why did Cicero believe that open voting, even though in writing, would reestablish the *auctoritas* of the *boni*, of men like Marcus Servilius?

If they are to help illuminate ancient politics – my sole interest at present in patron–client relations – the answers must be specific and concrete. Mantinea is rarely noticed and the brief passage in Xenophon is admittedly limited in its usefulness. Cicero's proposal for a revised voting procedure was only an idea, never introduced

---

[45] For what follows, see Nicolet (1970).

[46] Plutarch, *Aemilius Paulus* 31. The much longer account in Livy 45.35–9 ends in a lacuna in the manuscript, so that these words are absent. There can be little doubt that Polybius was the source for both Livy and Plutarch.

43

into practice. But Cleisthenes and the developments of the succeeding half-century are critical in this discussion and the massive scholarly analyses they have evoked are precisely where I had hoped to find answers, and failed.[47] No one can reasonably deny that Cleisthenes invented an ingeniously artificial scheme based on demes and tribes (one of a number of imaginative political inventions in Athens that we shall consider in subsequent chapters); that his scheme was accepted by the *demos* and survived not only until the end of Athenian democracy but several centuries beyond that, even under Roman rule; and that he and the *demos* saw in the scheme a necessary instrument in changing the political orientation, in giving the *demos* a greater share in public affairs (in Aristotle's words).[48] Only Aristotle offers a clue, no more than that, as to how this last was brought about, in his reference to breaking up old associations.

The traditional, and still dominant, explanation assumes that Cleisthenes was contending with a society which was tribally organized in the technical 'anthropological' sense. The aristocrats were, on this view, tribal chieftains – the terminology varies from language to language: clan, *Sippe*, *Stamm*, *société gentilice*, and so on – whose authority stemmed from, and rested on, that status. Remarkably, given its long and virtually unchallenged acceptance, that view is based on no Greek or Roman evidence, and indeed runs

---

[47] In a long chapter on Cleisthenes, Christian Meier (1980) rightly protests the absence of concreteness in previous discussions, yet he does not take into account the one great advance that modern scholarship has made on the subject, the study of the deme–tribe system 'on the ground' from archaeological and epigraphical evidence; see Traill (1975) with addenda by Rhodes (1980), and, for a survey of recent views, cf. J. Martin, 'Von Kleisthenes zu Ephialtes', *Chiron* 4 (1974) 5–42, at pp. 7–22.

[48] Herodotus and Aristotle were both firm that it was the *demos*, including the poor, whom Cleisthenes associated with his programme. In the two relevant chapters (20–1) of the *Constitution of Athens*, Aristotle uses the word *demos* four times and *to plethos* ('the multitude') four times, but never *to meson* ('the middle stratum'). Meier (1980) nevertheless asserts that Cleisthenes was concerned only with the middle stratum and that the poor were anyway indifferent, and he then calls that assertion a 'finding' (*Befund*) and builds his account on it. For a valuable and unique attempt to imagine how the complex scheme was planned and carried through, see A. Andrewes, 'Kleisthenes' Reform Bill', *Classical Quarterly* 27 (1977) 241–8. The added complication of a confused tradition that Cleisthenes also extended citizenship to some 'aliens' need not concern us; see most recently E. Grace, 'Aristotle on the "Enfranchisement of Aliens" by Cleisthenes (a Note)', *Klio* 56 (1974) 353–68.

counter to the evidence. In so far as it is not merely the by-product of a linear theory of human social evolution, it reflects a fundamental confusion between family and clan or tribe. Of course the family was the nuclear social unit in early archaic times, among the élite as among the peasantry (as it continued to be in later social systems, including our own). The question, however, is about the organization of the community as a whole, and it is in this area that the supposed kinship structure proves to be a fiction. Kinship, real or putative, is not what gave the aristocracy its hold over the common people.[49] Nor does it help to turn to the German favourite, *Gefolgschaft* (French *compagnonnage*). In so far as it is not a tautology – a following is a following (*Gefolgschaft*) – that notion injects anachronistic elements from feudal (or quasi-feudal) societies, with a strong military component, for which there is again no support and sufficient counter-proof in the evidence.[50]

If Greek and Roman aristocrats were neither tribal chieftains nor feudal war lords, then their power must have rested on something else, and I suggest the obvious, their wealth and the ways in which they could disburse it. I am willing to concede a role to prestige, charisma, *mos maiorum*, even control of cult centres, though Denis Roussel has rightly objected to 'representing the priest-citizens of the great sanctuaries of Attica in the image of the curates and bishops who in some modern states have often influenced the votes in their parishes or dioceses'.[51] I am also prepared to stress more strongly than many historians the importance of conflicting political and economic programmes (or measures) in fostering or pandering to the ambitions of élite political leaders.[52] However, the Graeco-Roman world would have been unique in history if personal patronage – the 'objective' element in the relationship between unequals – were not consciously deployed in support of the power structure. Cimon's practice shows that we need assume no such uniqueness.

Nor need we assume that Cimon was somehow unusual in his

---

[49] The question has been settled for Greece by Roussel (1976) and there is no doubt in my mind that his analysis fits the Roman picture as well. True, the Roman *gens*, unlike the Greek *genos*, was a lineage, but it was only an aristocratic lineage and had nothing in common with a clan or a tribe.

[50] Even the proponents of a mystical Roman *clientela*, mentioned above in n. 39, would be hard put to squeeze it under the *Gefolgschaft* rubric, though some have tried.

[51] Roussel (1976) 285n7.   [52] See ch. 5 below.

behaviour, despite the paucity of explicit documentation.[53] It has been demonstrated that members of the wealthiest census-class, the *pentakosiomedimnoi*, were widely scattered among the Attic demes: the 187 men known to have been on the three major financial boards in the second half of the fifth century B.C., a sufficient random-sample, came from 78 different demes, including some of the smallest and the most remote.[54] Though they did not necessarily reside in their demes, that was where their ancestral estates were located, where, if they wished, they could have exercised patronage. I myself have no doubt that some of them did so wish, on the model of Cimon or in other ways. Once we have exorcised the spectre of tribalism, together with such consequent errors as the notion that Cleisthenes substituted 'locality for birth' as the basis for political relationships and controls,[55] the whole tradition about archaic Athenian politics points to the deme, the neighbourhood, as the base from which political careers were launched through the deployment of wealth, through local patronage. The neighbourhood was the key, for example, to the struggle for power among leading aristocratic houses in the decades following Solon, which was brought to an end by the tyranny of Pisistratus.[56]

It is significant that of the few innovations by Pisistratus that have survived in the historical record, two were obviously designed to weaken the local power of the richer landowners by undermining major devices that fostered patron–client relations. Pisistratus set up

[53] The only parallel in the sources is a brief remark of the fourth-century B.C. historian Theopompus about Pisistratus (115F135 ap. Athenaeus 12.44,532F), who is there said to have opened his estates to everyone, not only to fellow-demesmen. Elsewhere (115F89 ap. Athenaeus 533A) Theopompus said the same of Cimon; his version is repeated by some later writers but was tacitly rejected by both Aristotle and Theophrastus (as quoted by Cicero, *De officiis* 2.64), whose source is unidentifiable. If my analysis of patronage is right, Aristotle's version is likely to be the correct one. Lysias 16.14 perhaps provides some confirmation. The material is assembled by Connor (1968) 24–38, who does not seem to envisage the patronage aspect.

[54] W. E. Thompson, 'The Regional Distribution of the Athenian Pentakosiomedimnoi', *Klio* 52 (1970) 437–51.

[55] D. W. Bradeen, 'The Trittyes in Cleisthenes' Reform', *Transactions of the American Philological Association* 86 (1955) 22–30, at p. 22.

[56] This struggle is conventionally discussed by historians under the rubric 'regionalism', but that introduces incorrect notions about economic differences among the 'regions'. For a detailed account of the discussion and a sensible analysis, see E. Kluwe, 'Bemerkungen zu den Diskussionen über die drei "Parteien" in Attika . . .', *Klio* 54 (1972) 101–24.

a revolving loan-fund for peasants and he created a board of thirty 'deme-judges' who went on circuit; the former measure made available an alternative source of loans, the latter weakened, if it did not remove, the jurisdictional power of the local aristocracy.[57] Pisistratus was a 'tyrant', but that is irrelevant in the immediate context: anyone, individual or group, seeking to develop and strengthen the *polis* was compelled in this early stage to contend with the traditional hold of the aristocracy in the demes, and that could be done only by offering alternative forms of subsistence crisis insurance. In that respect, Pericles was a direct heir of Pisistratus: he reestablished the apparently defunct board of deme judges (Aristotle, *Constitution of Athens* 26.3) and he instituted a long series of measures giving financial assistance to the poor from state funds, normally not by direct grants but by payment for services to the state. Great changes had taken place in Athens between the death of Pisistratus and the leadership of Pericles, notably the creation of a maritime empire and the establishment of democracy. Hence their techniques differed sharply, but in a basic sense they were trying to overcome the same danger to the political structure of Athens, the rural poverty which was a breeding-ground for aristocratic patronage. Stated differently, Pisistratus' concern was with a military threat by his defeated but not powerless aristocratic rivals, whereas Pericles had to compete with men like Cimon for the votes in the Council and Assembly of all the citizenry, rich, middle-class and poor, who had gained a direct share in government.[58]

What, then, did Cleisthenes contribute? How did his 'mixing everyone up' in his newly created tribal structure block the powerful individuals from making use of their patronage networks for political ends? We can only guess because we have so little information. The key must lie in the Council of 500, the *boule*, in which every tribe had fifty members and every deme at least one, and in which repeated membership was prohibited. This compul-

---

[57] Aristotle, *Constitution of Athens* 16.2–5. This is one time when I am compelled to agree with Aristotle's modern critics. Pisistratus' motive, he writes, was to keep the peasantry at home, away from the city. That is an unwarranted attribution to the tyrant of one of Aristotle's favourite political judgments: e.g. *Politics* 1318b9–16.

[58] It cannot be stressed too sharply that the struggle was for control at the centre, not, as, e.g., Davies (1971) 311 presents it, one between Cimon the 'local dynast' and Pericles the 'national politician'.

sory geographical distribution of members of the Council seems to have reduced sharply the range of influence that local patrons could have exercised. Once the councillors were chosen by lot – the date is controversial and apparently unresolvable – direct control over the Council by patrons was further minimized. However, the Assembly remained untouched by the deme-tribe mechanism; every citizen remained free to attend, and his vote, given openly, was the equal of every other.

There were means of overcoming some of the effects of 'mixing up' through horizontal and vertical alliances among patrons, thereby pooling the voting strength of their supporters. The existence of such alliances (though little of the operational detail) is easier to discover in Rome, with its sharply contested elections to high office (largely unknown in Greek city-states), where the situation was complicated by the vastly greater extent of territory and eventually by the increasingly arbitrary assignment of newly incorporated areas to the existing tribes. Memorize the tribal map of Italy – that is the advice given to Cicero, who was standing for the consulship, in a pamphlet, the *Commentariolum*, attributed to his brother Quintus. The point is then clarified in the pamphlet itself and in other contemporary sources. Electoral success required assiduous cultivation of key individuals in each tribe who were in a position to bring out enough voters to guarantee the unitary vote of the tribe.[59] 'Name any tribe', Cicero himself said in defending Gnaeus Plancius against a charge of corruption in his election to the aedileship, 'and I will tell you through whom he carried it' (*Oration for Plancius* 48). Again I must insist that Rome (this time) would have been unique in history if what I have called the objective element in patronage were not a significant element in the procedure. In another speech for the defence in a case of electoral corruption, Cicero meets the accusation that the large crowds who escorted his client had been bribed to do so: first he denies that there was any bribery, then he generalizes (*For Murena* 70), 'The common people (*homines tenues*) have only one way of either *earning or repaying benefits* at the hands of our order, and that is to render us the service of escorting us when we

---

[59] The practice in the final decades of the Republic is described in detail by Taylor (1949) ch. 3. Virtually all the evidence comes from that abnormal period but there is no reason to think that electoral practice was essentially different in the preceding two centuries except that the scale was a much reduced one.

are candidates for office'. The words I have written in italics are to be understood literally.

What I have been trying to suggest, in sum, is that inquiry into the ancient state and government needs to be lowered from the stratosphere of rarefied concepts, by a consideration not only of ideology, of 'national' pride and patriotism, of DER STAAT, of the glories and miseries of war, but also of the material relations among the citizens or classes of citizens as much as those more commonly noticed between the state and the citizens. The picture will then require still further articulation. We shall have to allow for the large leavening of citizens who were indifferent to politics, and for those who successfully flouted both the *mos maiorum* and the more formalized rules of behaviour. We shall also have to consider, and seek to explain, the failures, not only the unstable city-states but also those whose stability was eventually undermined. Of our three exemplars, Athens, Sparta and Rome, one (Athens) did not lose its stability but was destroyed as an independent city-state by the superior force of Macedon; the other two were victims, each in its way, of their own military successes. Only a more concrete inquiry into politics and political conflict may suggest explanations.

3

POLITICS

In an oft repeated story Plutarch tells how, on one occasion in Athens while the voting was under way for an ostracism, an illiterate rustic approached a man and asked him to inscribe his potsherd (*ostrakon*) for him with the name Aristides. The man asked what harm Aristides had done him, and received the reply, 'None whatever. I don't even know the man, but I am fed up with hearing him called "The Just" everywhere.' Whereupon Aristides, for the man was he of course, duly entered his own name as requested (*Aristides 7.6*). An edifying tale, but my interest is in the willingness of historians to accept it as true and to draw from it wide-ranging conclusions about Aristides, about ostracism, and about Athenian democracy. Some had doubts about the image of Athenian political leaders as noble gentlemen who would not sully themselves with such low forms of behaviour as canvassing peasants and shopkeepers (only good political leaders, I need hardly add, not demagogues like Cleon). The sceptics have now scored an unexpected triumph. Excavations since the last war have uncovered, chiefly in the potters' quarter, more than eleven thousand ostraca with names inscribed on them.[1] Most were obviously dumped in quantity following the completion of one or another ostracism. However, one batch of 190 found on the west slope of the Acropolis all bore the name of Themistocles, written in a small number of hands, clearly prepared beforehand for distribution among potential voters but in the end not used. There is no way of knowing what proportion of the other eleven thousand sherds had been similarly inscribed in advance. Nor is there any way of telling whether Plutarch's story about Aristides is true or not. Many of his stories are moralizing fictions, and it is virtually inconceivable that the batch of unused Themistocles ostraca constituted a unique instance of this tactic in the whole history of ostracism. We must decide from the probabilities, and Plutarch does not persuade me

---

[1] R. Thomsen, *The Origin of Ostracism* (Copenhagen 1972), pp. 84–108.

50

that Athenian politics had a moral purity unknown in any other political society.[2] Historians of Rome have a harder time because they have at their disposal that unique collection of ancient documents, the letters of Cicero. There one reads such things as the following, written to his friend and confidant Atticus (1.2.1) in July 65 B.C. 'At the moment I am proposing to defend my fellow-candidate Catiline [for the consulship]. We have the jury we want, with full cooperation from the prosecution. If he is acquitted I hope he will be more inclined to work with me in the campaign.'[3] Catiline faced trial for extortion while governor of the province of Africa. He was acquitted without the help of Cicero, who in the end failed to take on the case for reasons we do not know. Two years later Cicero took the lead in destroying the Catilinarian conspiracy. That is also illuminating. But such texts and such situations do not warrant the headlong rush to shelter under the rubric 'corruption'. Canvassing, persuasion, exchange of services, rewards and benefits, alliances and deals are the essential techniques of politics in real life, in every known political society, and the line between corruption and non-corruption is not only extremely difficult to draw but also shifts according to the observer's ethical system. Not everyone agrees with Plato.

By 'politics' I mean something specific and much narrower than, for example, Michael Oakeshott's 'the activity of attending to the general arrangements of a set of people whom chance or choice has brought together'.[4] That definition, which is widely shared, embraces every conceivable group from a family or club or loose tribal unit to the most omnipotent autocratic monarchy or tyranny, and I am unable to find any analytical or otherwise meaningful use for it. Three distinctions seem to me to be necessary. The first is between states and the manifold groupings which exist within a state, social, economic, educational or whatever. I have no concern

---

[2] As an indication of how deeply the traditional view has become embedded, note W. den Boer, *Private Morality in Greece and Rome* (*Mnemosyne*, Supp. 57, 1979), p. 184: 'It is said that ostraca with the name of Themistocles were widespread before the vote which condemned him and his policy. This was a fraud which undoubtedly occurred, but it cannot be said to have been general.' For a recent demonstration of Plutarch's unreliability as a source for fifth-century Athens, see A. Andrewes, 'The Opposition to Perikles', *Journal of Hellenic Studies* 98 (1978) 1–8.

[3] Translated by D. R. Shackleton Bailey.   [4] M. Oakeshott, in Laslett (1956) 2.

with such metaphorical uses as 'academic politics'. The second is between states in which decisions are binding and enforceable and pre-state structures in which they are not. The third is between states in which one man or a junta has the absolute power of decision regardless of how much advice may be sought beforehand, and those in which *binding* decisions are reached by discussion and argument and ultimately by voting. The discussion may be restricted to only one sector of the community members, as in an oligarchy – I do not narrow my definition to democracies – or primarily to elected representatives or to decision about a limited range of issues, but it is essential that the decision be more than advisory. These are the reasons for my chronological limits, and particularly for my exclusion of Rome under the emperors. Where the principle *Quod principi placuit legis habet vigorem* ('What the emperor decides has the force of statute') prevails, even if only in spirit, there is government by antechamber, not by chamber, and therefore there can be no politics in my sense. That is to say, although there was discussion in the Principate, the final and effectively unrestrained power of decision on matters of policy rested with one man, not with voters (not even with the hundreds comprising the Senate).

There were admittedly large grey areas not easily classifiable, for example, the Seleucid cities or the cities in the Roman Empire, with their privilege of self-government on a narrowly defined local level. I exclude the latter from this inquiry because their politics are of interest in studying the social psychology of an élite under an overriding autocracy but not sufficiently in the study of political behaviour. One may compare two documents – whether or not they are purely literary creations is irrelevant – a short dialogue between Socrates and young Glaucon in Xenophon's *Memorabilia* (3.6) and a long essay, *Political Precepts*, written by Plutarch probably about A.D. 100. Both ostensibly offer advice to an upper-class youngster with political ambitions. Whereas Socrates concentrates on the need for detailed knowledge – about public finance, military resources, defence, the silver mines, food supply[5] – Plutarch goes on at endless length, sententiously, with many quotations from Greek and Latin writers and many stories, all about decorous behaviour, honesty, a moderate way of life, the

---

[5] Cf. Aristotle, *Rhetoric* 1359b19–60a37.

choice of the right friends and patrons, and above all rhetoric. I can find little in the essay about substantive matters even in the past, and nothing that illuminates politics past or present. That the difference between the two is not a matter of two different personalities or temperaments but a reflection of two wholly different situations is, I believe, signalled by Plutarch himself midway in the piece when he writes (*Moralia* 813D–E): 'When you enter into any post you must not only consider the calculation of Pericles . . ., "Take care Pericles, you are ruling free men, you are ruling Greeks, citizens of Athens"; but you must also say to yourself, "You who hold office are a subject, in a *polis* controlled by proconsuls, by Caesar's procurators."'

Politics in our sense rank among the rarer of human activities in the pre-modern world. In effect, they were a Greek invention, more correctly perhaps, the separate inventions of the Greeks and of the Etruscans and/or Romans. Presumably there were other early political communities in the Near East, among the Phoenicians at any rate, who then carried their institutions to Carthage in the west. The only non-Greek state included by Aristotle in his collection of 158 monographs about individual 'constitutions' was Carthage. That work is lost, though some of the information survives in the *Politics* (especially 1272b24–73b26), and I can find no ground for thinking that there was any significant diffusion from the Phoenicians to the Greeks or Etruscans (who, I take it, laid the foundations on which Roman political institutions were developed). How much influence the early Greek communities in Sicily and Italy may have had on the Etruscans and Romans in their formative stages is a much debated and unanswerable question; really an unimportant question: no answer will throw light on the different ways in which politics and political institutions developed in the Greek and Roman spheres.

I stress the originality chiefly for its corollary, the iron compulsion both Greeks and Romans were under to be continuously inventive, as new and often unanticipated problems or difficulties arose that had to be resolved without the aid of precedents or models. Hence the familiar list of 'odd' devices and institutions, such as the Cleisthenic tribes, ostracism and the *graphe paranomon* (to which we shall return) in Athens, the tribunician 'veto' and especially the extraordinary voting procedure of the *comitia centuriata* in Rome. Badian has correctly said of the latter that 'anyone who has studied the reformed Roman *comitia centuriata* will think nothing impossible'.[6] David Hume found it difficult to comprehend the 'singular and seemingly absurd' *graphe paranomon*, an Athenian procedure introduced in the course of the fifth century B.C. whereby any citizen could prosecute another for having made an 'illegal proposal' in the Assembly, *even when the sovereign Assembly had approved it.*[7] Such devices are interesting not only in themselves, as examples of the remarkable range of human inventiveness in the political field, but also (and even more) in their individual histories, as case-studies of the ways in which institutions can be turned and twisted, sometimes out of all recognition, once they have been introduced into the political armoury. I must insist once again that it is wrong to approach this topic as little more than a story of demagogy, popular corruption, decline and breakdown, for it is a central thread in the history of ancient politics, easily paralleled, though perhaps not often so picturesquely, in the history of modern politics.

We are not helped much by the sources. The Greeks and Romans invented politics, and, as everyone knows, they also invented political history, or rather history as the history of war and politics. But what everyone knows is imprecise: historians in antiquity wrote the history of policy, which is not the same thing as politics; they wrote primarily about foreign policy, concerning themselves with the *mechanics* of policy-making (apart from speeches in Senate or Assembly) only in moments of acute conflict turning into civil war. Consider Thucydides. Once we eliminate his set-piece on the civil war in Corcyra and other, brief civil-war narratives, the ideal-type speeches, and the account in his unrevised last book of the oligarchical coup of 411, there are only the most incidental remarks about politics, usually introduced in order to express a moral judgment (and in the appropriate language): for example, his throwaway remark (8.73.3) that one Hyperbolus 'had been ostracized not because of fear of his power or prestige but because he was a rogue and a disgrace to the *polis*'. That is absurd in operational political terms, and Plutarch of all people pointed to the reality in his circumstantial tale (*Nicias* 11) of how, probably in 416 B.C., when the conflict between Alcibiades and Nicias had reached such a

[6] E. Badian, 'Archons and *Strategoi*', *Antichthon* 5 (1971) 1–34, at p. 19.
[7] 'Hume's Early Memoranda, 1729–1740', ed. E. C. Mossner, *Journal of the History of Ideas* 9 (1948) 492–518, no. 237.

pitch that one or the other was likely to be ostracized, the two joined forces and succeeded in persuading their supporters to vote to ostracize Hyperbolus. This tale, unlike the one about Aristides the Just, has a genuine aura of plausibility. Had it been taken more seriously by historians, and not pounced on as just another sign of popular degeneracy, a 'sinister intrigue',[8] the prefabricated Themistocles ostraca might not have come as such a shock.

There is nothing terribly arcane or difficult about the history of ostracism, apart from the chronological puzzles that occupy the bulk of the extensive modern literature on the subject. It was introduced when the Athenians introduced a democratic system, following the decades of the Pisistratid tyranny. With characteristic and unavoidable inventiveness, it was decided that the risk of another tyrant could be reduced by expelling an overly successful and popular leader for ten years if a minimum of 6,000 votes were cast in a formal procedure. Soon enough, politicians found ostracism to be a useful device for decapitating the opposition – a neat illustration of one implication of an oral culture: remove a man physically from the state and he has no lines of communication with the citizenry. But it was a weapon with a dangerous double edge; so it was used sparingly – there is no certain instance between 443 B.C. and the ostracism of Hyperbolus in 416 – and after 416 it was allowed to die a quiet death. In contrast, the *graphe paranomon*, originally designed to give the Athenians an opportunity to reconsider a possibly rushed Assembly decision, proved to be a useful weapon in the in-fighting within the leadership circles and it was employed with some frequency as the years went on.[9]

The epithet 'sinister intrigue', in so far as it is not just donnish highmindedness about politics (all politics, ancient or modern), is a fair example of the unfortunate habit of allowing the sources to lead the historian. For classical Greece it is sufficiently well known that enough of the main sources – among the historians as well as the philosophers and pamphleteers – were hostile to prevailing political

---

[8] Hignett (1952) 165. For a proper approach to the Hyperbolus affair, see Andrewes' commentary on the Thucydides passage and Connor (1971) 79–84.

[9] H. J. Wolff, *Normenkontrolle und Gesetzesbegriff in der attischen Demokratie* (Sitzungsberichte der Heidelberger Akad. d. Wiss., Phil.-hist. Klasse 2, 1970), replaces all previous accounts of the *graphe paranomon*. The 39 known cases (some uncertain) between 415 and 322 B.C., of which perhaps half ended in acquittals, are summarized by M. H. Hansen, *The Sovereignty of the People's Court in Athens . . .* (Odense Univ. Classical Studies 4, 1974), pp. 28–43.

practice and expressed their dislike in moral terms. I need not proliferate instances: that would not strengthen my plea for brushing aside the moralizing veil in the search for political reality. Nor need I repeat the argument for Rome. Despite the differences, notably that Roman institutions, heavily weighted in favour of the rich and the few, did not draw the fire of Roman writers or Greek commentators, the literature has the same concentration, the same lack of any sustained interest in politics (always excepting Cicero's letters, to be contrasted on this score with his theoretical writings and his historical allusions). The sharp dispute preceding the decision to destroy Carthage in the so-called Third Punic War (149–146 B.C.) is a sufficient example: although the disagreements within the Roman ruling circle 'must have been a highly significant factor in the internal politics of Rome . . . few traces of it can be discerned'.[10]

Nor, I trust, need I waste much time on the fundamental difference between constitutional law and politics. The habit of falling into the constitutional-law trap is perhaps more common among Roman historians, thanks to the great corpus of Roman juristic literature and thanks even more to that towering intellectual construct, Mommsen's *Römisches Staatsrecht*. So there is the unending debate about the nature and limits of the Senate's authority over the magistrates, as if they were not the same people, drawn from a small circle of the *nobilitas*, and did not talk to each other before any formal steps were taken.[11] Greek history is not immune: a recent lengthy monograph about the relative roles of Council and Assembly in Athenian legislation sets out explicitly to locate the 'legislative or decision-making process' and claims to have done so by a purely formal (and faulty) analysis of the 'parliamentary' *mechanics* alone.[12]

Of course the constitution, written or unwritten, provided the framework within which political activity was carried on. That is almost too banal to bear putting into words. Nothing has been

---

[10] Astin (1967) 53.
[11] For a review of the discussion, see W. Kunkel, 'Magistratische Gewalt und Senatsherrschaft', in *Aufstieg und Niedergang der römischen Welt*, ed. H. Temporini I 2 (1972), pp. 3–22.
[12] R. A. DeLaix, *Probouleusis at Athens* (Berkeley 1973). On the flaws even within its limited scope, see the review by H. W. Pleket in *Mnemosyne*, 4th ser., 31 (1978) 328–33.

written about more frequently than Greek and Roman constitutions and constitutional history; the details are readily available in standard handbooks, textbooks and monographs, and I shall not attempt to go over the ground here. However, a number of general points are too essential for the study of politics to be left unsaid (and some specific points will have to be reexamined in the next chapter).

One must begin with a generalization: every city-state government consisted of at least a larger assembly (and usually of only one), a smaller council or councils and a number of officials rotated among the eligible men, most often on an annual basis. The composition of these bodies, their method of selection, their powers, the names by which they were known, all varied greatly, in place and in time, but the tripartite system was so ubiquitous that one may think of it as synonymous with city-state government. The earliest available documentation comes from such scattered places as Dreros in Crete and Sparta before 600 B.C., Athens probably soon after, Chios in the middle of the sixth century, and by 500 B.C. a backward region of Greece, Locris, as well as Rome. No implications should be drawn from the list itself, other than its randomness: we know about Sparta, Athens and Rome because they are Sparta, Athens and Rome, with a strong tradition that dominates the literature; we know about Dreros, Chios and Locris from the accidental survival of brief inscriptions on stone or bronze and their information does not extend beyond the mere fact of the existence of assembly, council and officials.[13] How long before the first surviving document the system may have been installed in any community is unknown, and for my purposes unimportant, just as it does not matter whether or not one accepts the tradition that Solon first established a council in Athens.

Variations in the details often led to major consequences, whether intended or not. It is, in particular, impossible to make a comparative study without noticing one fundamental difference between Rome and Athens. In the latter most offices were restricted to one annual term, membership of the Council to two, with the notable exception of the office of *strategos*, from the early fifth century B.C. much the most prestigious in the state, to which one was elected (not chosen by lot) and could be reelected without limit. In Rome,

---

[13] The texts from Dreros, Chios and Locris are Meiggs/Lewis (1969) nos. 2, 8 and 13, respectively.

by contrast, all offices were in principle restricted to a single one-year tenure (a rule that was violated in pra tice but not significantly before the last century of the Republi(), whereas the council, the Senate, was a permanent body with what amounted to life tenure. Hence a politically ambitious Athenian could stand for repeated election to the *strategia* as an important though not essential base from which to operate, whereas his Roman counterpart was prohibited from doing anything analogous. Once he had been consul, a Roman could exert political influence solely through the Senate or through informal channels.

The tripartite constitutional structure rested on the need for efficiency, or at least for a workable machinery; its establishment did not arise out of an idea of the separation of powers in the sense developed by Montesquieu (though such theorists as Aristotle (*Politics* 1297b35–1301a15) adumbrated the idea after the fact). Nor was there the modern separation of powers in the judicial sphere: there was of course a court machinery, but it overlapped with the rest, in the right of a council or assembly to sit as a trial court for major cases or, at the other extreme, in the plenipotentiary power of magistrates to penalize certain categories of offenders.[14]

In principle there was also no separation between the civil and the military departments of government. Not only was the army (though not usually the navy) a citizens' militia but the commanding officers were the ranking civilian officials. Spartan exceptionalism in this sphere was merely the extension of a universal city-state institution to its ultimate logical conclusion. The ten Athenian *strategoi* were elected annually and their roster in the fifth century includes the best known political leaders of the time, chosen to hold the highest military office because of their political influence, not the other way round. In Rome, Polybius tells us (6.19.4), no one could hold a political office until he had served in ten annual military campaigns. There has been scholarly controversy and a fair amount of special pleading round this simple statement, but there can be no doubt about its basic correctness, and surely not about the duty of consuls to lead the armies in the field. Given the regularity of war in Roman republican history, that meant that military command was a normal part of every consul's duties.[15]

---

[14] Nippel (1980) replaces previous literature on the subject.
[15] Harris (1979) 10–41 gives an excellent detailed account in a section entitled 'The Aristocracy and War'.

This identity of civilian and military roles existed in principle, as I have said, and the notable fact is not that there were eventually important departures in practice, but that the principle was clung to so tenaciously. During the Peloponnesian War, Sparta was compelled to break the rule that the two kings were the commanders of field armies simply because there were more than two armies in action at the same time – but the rule was not abandoned. The fourth century B.C. saw considerable employment of professional generals and mercenary soldiers by the Greek city-states, but the citizen militia remained the basic military arm. Notably, however, in Athens such political leaders as Eubulus or Demosthenes[16] no longer found it essential for their status to command armies, as had Pericles and Cleon in the previous century. As for Rome, the profound transformation which eventually saw the traditional militia acquire under such commanders as Marius, Sulla, Pompey and Caesar something of the character of a private army (though not in a strict sense), is too familiar to require any elaboration. But the fact that Rome had conquered Italy, Carthage and parts of Spain before the change set in, relatively late in the second century B.C., must be underscored.

Change is of course what the history of politics is about; in the final analysis, change in one or another respect was both the objective and the consequence of political disagreements and conflicts. We must therefore turn from broad constitutional outlines to the important variables. The first of these is size. In a very large majority of the Greek city-states the adult male citizens numbered under 10,000 and, in many, under 5,000; the same was true of the communities in Italy which Rome took over in the course of two or three centuries. One assumes that political activity in such little units, in which the entire citizenry could in fact be brought together in an assembly, was somehow different in its tone, its quality, from the activity in Athens, with its thirty-five or forty thousand citizens, and in Rome which became far larger. Unfortunately the assumption cannot be tested: the only smaller state about which there is useful evidence is the untypical Sparta, and it would be folly to extrapolate from Sparta to, say, Mytilene or Sicyon or Capua.

The relative scale of all this has constantly to be borne in mind.

---

[16] The fourth-century orator and statesman Demosthenes is not to be confused with the fifth-century general of the same name mentioned later in this chapter.

Our best guess is that the total population of the Roman empire at its peak, at the beginning of the Christian era, was equal to, or a bit greater than, that of the United Kingdom today. That was also the time of maximum urbanization in antiquity, yet there were not half a dozen cities larger than Belfast or Miami, not one (other than Rome) as populous as Leeds or Milwaukee. However, it is not the totals or modern comparisons that matter in the present context but the relative capacities to fulfil ancient expectations. In a world of low technology, predominantly small landholdings, a stratified social structure and an indefatigable appetite for local wars, independent communities with a citizen population under ten thousand were chronically unstable; they lacked the resources and the manpower to protect themselves from the social and political consequences of natural disasters, such as a succession of famine years, and of persistent armed conflict. Hence – though this is admittedly only an impression, given our inadequate evidence – the frequency of a breakdown in politics in favour of open civil war, often enough accompanied by betrayal of the city to one or another more powerful state.[17] That was a price paid for the incorporation of the lower classes into the political community. Only the larger states were able to escape, not only by the use of force externally but also by the ability to exercise their greater resources 'peacefully', for example by control of maritime routes. There can be no better illustration of the close interrelationship between domestic and foreign affairs in shaping the politics within any state.[18]

It would be difficult to overestimate the impact of war on ancient politics. The unparalleled Roman record of war and conquest should not blind us to the fact that there were also few years in the history of most Greek city-states (of Sparta and Athens in particular), and hardly any years in succession, without some military engagements. We must also bear constantly in mind that the brunt of the fighting was borne by citizen militias; furthermore, that in many Greek states (including Athens and Sparta) and in early Rome, the men who made the decisions to fight were largely those

---

[17] On the inevitable political 'oscillation' in small city-states, see Heuss (1973) 19–24.

[18] Acknowledgement should be made of the contribution by Otto Hintze towards a proper appreciation by modern historians of this dialectical relationship; see especially Hintze (1962) 34–40, 53–6. This dialectic is a central theme of Heuss (1973); cf. Schuller (1979).

who went straight into battle themselves, from the commanders down the social and economic scale to the men of fairly modest property who constituted the heavy infantry, and sometimes even down to the poor who manned the warships. The variables immediately begin to proliferate. The first distinction is between conquest-states, those which subjected relatively extensive territory or a relatively large number of previously independent communities to their authority, and the others, which did not. An immediate consequence was change, distortion and sometimes destruction of the governmental system and the politics of the subject-communities. Schematically stated, imperial states favoured, and often imposed, preferred constitutional systems on their subjects and intervened politically or militarily in order to achieve the desired result: tyranny where tyrants were the conquerors, as in Sicily; democracy in the Athenian power-sphere; oligarchy where Sparta or Rome was the controlling power.[19] At the receiving end, in the subject-cities, there was a readiness on the part of the different factions to summon external military support, not only in conflicts over the form of government (oligarchy or democracy) but also in power struggles within oligarchies.[20] As usual, the sources let us down; primarily concerned with the imperial states, they provide no more than an occasional hint about the politics in the subordinate communities as these gravitated about the pressures and demands exerted upon them from outside.[21] More precisely, ancient authors restrict their information to the constitutional issues and to the bare bones of assassination, exile and confiscation. The model statement is that of Thucydides (3.82.1) in his great set-piece on the civil war in Corcyra in 427 B.C.: 'in wartime, when each side could always count on alliances that would harm the other and benefit itself, it was easy for those wishing a revolution to call in help'.

Thucydides' generalization can be illustrated many times over

---

[19] In the case of Sparta I refer here only to the 'allied' states in the Peloponnesian League, not to the Messenians who were reduced to helotage, with decisive effects on the Spartan system briefly noted in ch. 1. See Finley (1975) ch. 10; on the Peloponnesian League, de Ste Croix (1972) ch. 4.

[20] That intra-oligarchic struggles were often the occasion for external interference is brought out by I. A. F. Bruce, 'The Democratic Revolution at Rhodes', *Classical Quarterly*, n.s. 11 (1961) 166–70, and 'Internal Politics and the Outbreak of the Corinthian War', *Emerita* 28 (1960) 75–86.

[21] See generally Finley (1978*a*) 11–14, (1978*b*) 124–6.

throughout the period we are discussing, but with a monotonous sameness and a lack of meaningful detail about the politics of the manoeuvres. Only the political feedback in the more powerful, the conquering states can be documented, and that story is anything but uniform or monotonous. Sparta was of course unique. A citizen-body that was also a full-time army under the command of hereditary kings, maintained by a large helot population, was in a different situation in all respects from the citizenry of any other *polis*. There is too much that we do not know. It is not very helpful, for example, to be told by Aristotle, with no details, that the kings were compelled to court (*demagogein*) the ephors, that the latter were elected annually by a 'childish' method, that the Council of Elders were selected for life by manipulation.[22] No ancient author discusses the psychology of an army, trained in obedience from childhood, when it met as an assembly to decide between alternative proposals put to it by kings and ephors. We can safely guess that the pressures were different from those operating in an Athenian (or any other) assembly, but we can say no more. Yet we know that at times there were sharp disagreements over policy that had to be resolved politically.[23] As usual, the available accounts are restricted to military and foreign affairs, but the abortive revolt of Cinadon in 397 B.C. reveals a long-standing domestic crisis. As land ownership became heavily concentrated, more and more Spartiates were deprived of full citizenship status, with disastrous military consequences. Within two generations of Sparta's final success, the defeat of Athens in the Peloponnesian War, Sparta was reduced to a relatively minor city-state. There are signs of a trend to quasi-private armies and military monarchy, but the territorial and demographic resources were too slight.

Rome was unique in a different way because she was a relentless conquest-state from the beginning of her recorded history. The combination of, on the one hand, territorial acquisition and continuing peasant (citizen) settlement on confiscated land with, on the other hand, retention of a city-state framework and a measure of popular participation in government gave a peculiarly Roman stamp to every aspect of her history, society and politics.[24] Athens began

---

[22] *Politics* 1270b14, b28, 1306a18, respectively.

[23] For what we know, see A. Andrewes, 'The Government of Classical Sparta', in Badian (1966) 1–20; cf. D. M. Lewis, *Sparta and Persia* (Leiden 1977) ch. 2.

[24] See the excellent brief statement by Brunt (1971a) ch. 1.

with a larger territorial base – how the whole of Attica became a single city-state is an unresolved puzzle of early Athenian history – but in her imperial phase, in the fifth century B.C., she acquired a tribute-paying empire without annexing territory, though some land was confiscated for Athenian settlement. The difference had a sharp impact on size: Athens reached her ultimate peak in territory and population in the middle of the fifth century, yet was exceeded by Rome in territory on a scale of at least ten to one and in population perhaps by eight to one by the end of the third century B.C. And Rome continued to grow steadily in both respects for a long time thereafter.

Such a difference in magnitude could not have been without effect on politics. Indeed, so central is the conquest side of Roman history that we shall be returning to it repeatedly. Most obvious, perhaps, was its impact on the constitution and functioning of the political élite, on the selection and behaviour of political leaders. On this subject I do not find it helpful to employ either the conventional labels, democracy and oligarchy, or such refinements as the modern favourites, 'moderate' and 'radical' democracy. Politics are by their nature competitive, and the first distinction is between communities in which the competition is closed to a property-owning sector of the citizenry – oligarchies in the narrow sense – and those in which the poorer classes have some right of participation. Unfortunately, the information is lacking for a meaningful discussion of politics in the oligarchic Greek or Italian states; bits in Aristotle's *Politics* or in the historians indicate that their politics could be sharp and nasty, but they do not tell us much more. Only Athens and Rome lend themselves to analysis, and, for all their differences, they had in common an element of popular participation. Hence the political leaders, whoever they were and however they acquired their status, were compelled not only to manoeuvre among themselves but also to manoeuvre so as to secure popular support for various purposes. That is politics, and the tendency among historians to stress the lack of initiative among the mass of the citizenry and then to conclude that they therefore counted for little 'in reality' evades all the questions.

That political leadership was monopolized by the wealthier sector of the citizenry throughout the city-state era is well established, and some of the explanation has already been suggested. There were psychological reasons emanating from a traditionally hierarchical society with its firmly developed ideology of *nomos* or *mos maiorum*. There were strong financial reasons, too: the wealthier classes bore such costs of government and war as could not be transferred to the conquered people and subjects; munificence, public and private, became both an obligation on and a tool of the men who aspired to leadership, in Rome on an accelerating standard; leisure was required not only for political activity as such but also for the development of necessary skills, oratorical in particular, and for the acquisition of expert knowledge (in a world that relied heavily on oral communication and that lacked a bureaucratic apparatus).

Politics at the leadership level, in short, was a full-time activity, a way of life. And for that reason to say that there were 'families that had a tradition of involvement in public affairs and whose scions were encouraged or expected to take part in politics'[25] is true but only part of the truth. Every individual had to *choose* to devote himself to politics, and then he had to make his way: family gave him a headstart and constant backing but he himself had to run the course, a permanent obstacle-race, throughout his political life. The obstacles were placed in his way by his competitors in the struggle for leadership and the risks were formidable. Many scions of the families with a political tradition were either uninterested in politics or were failures at it. For Athens that is implied in a negative way by the shift in the leadership after the death of Pericles from traditional 'aristocratic' families to men who are becoming known among modern historians, on a rather poor analogy with Roman *novi homines*, as 'new politicians'.

In fact we have no way of counting heads. Too few political figures have survived in the historical record: some of the men whose names appear most often in the ostraca I mentioned earlier are otherwise unrecorded, and there are too many ostraca for them

---

[25] Connor (1971) 10. Less cautious writers go much further. A fanciful reconstruction of Athenian factional politics in the 480s has recently been built on the supposition that membership of a leading *genos* automatically imposed its own *de facto* political recognition on the aspiring young Athenian statesman, long before, that is, he achieved final inclusion in the magisterial ranks: G. M. F. Williams, 'The Kerameikos Ostraka', *Zeitschrift für Papyrologie und Epigraphik* 31 (1980), at pp. 106–7. The reference is to Cimon, aged twenty-one at most on his father's death in 489. It rests on nothing more than the conventional modern (not ancient) *genos*-mythology and is easily falsified: see F. Bourriot, *Recherches sur la nature du génos* (2 vols., Lille and Paris 1976).

to be dismissed as the Kilroys who turn up on voting-papers today – Menon the son of Menekleides, for example, with nearly 700 ostraca, or Callixenus son of Aristonymos with more than 250.[26] Our Roman prosopographical information is much more complete and seems to show a narrower oligarchy. I need cite only one set of well-known figures: between 232 and 133 B.C. the 200 consuls came from 58 aristocratic lineages (*gentes*), and of these, 159 came from 26 lineages, 99 from only ten lineages.[27] Yet even in the hundred-year period there were scions of the dominant families who failed to attain the consulship, there were 'new men' who entered the charmed circle, and, most important, only a minority of consuls were in effect political leaders.

But the latter, too, no matter how incompetent or indifferent to politics, had *imperium* during their year in office, as did the praetors. Cicero was merely codifying long accepted Roman doctrine when, in the opening pages of the third book of the *Laws*, he insisted that *imperium* was essential by nature for justice and orderly existence. It 'can truly be said', he continued, 'that the magistrate is articulate law (*lex loquens*), the law a silent magistrate'. Hence obedience to the magistrates is a necessary condition of a just society: the root-sense of *imperium* is 'order', 'command', with an unmistakably military overtone. Similarly, the 'centuries' of the centuriate assembly were military units in origin, and they, like *imperium*, bring us back to the beginning of the Republic, to the conquest-state and to the inseparability of military and civilian leadership. The visual symbols of *imperium* were the *fasces* (bundles of rods and axes bound together by red thongs) carried by lictors, always in attendance on consuls and praetors, a permanent reminder to Roman contemporaries of the military basis of civic

---

[26] In the register of propertied families in Davies (1971), Kallixenos is 9688 VII; Menon does not appear because the material was not then available. This implication from the ostraca had already been drawn by Connor (1968) 124–7, when only 1,500 were known.

[27] H. H. Scullard, *Roman Politics 220–150 B.C.* (2 ed., Oxford 1973), p. 11. Scullard speaks of 'families' and that is misleading, as Brunt (forthcoming) points out: 'it is uncertain if they [the members of a *gens*] had ever been connected by blood, and sometimes clear that even when they had common ancestors, their relationship (unless cemented by a marriage) had become very remote'. Graeco-Roman comparisons are weakened because Greek families were more nuclear than the Roman *gentes*, because the Romans made more use of adoption for political purposes, and because the Greek *polis* had no office-holding focus like the annual consulship or praetorship.

authority; Romans needed no learned gloss to make the connection.[28]

There was nothing comparable in the Greek city-states (with the possible and at best partial exception of the two hereditary kings in Sparta). Nor did the Greeks develop an institution like the formal triumph, a prize that Livy (30.15.12) called 'the most magnificent distinction' that could be awarded in Rome. The triumph was not awarded lightly; that is to say, an application normally required political manoeuvring for a successful outcome and it often led to debates in the Senate and sometimes outside.[29] Like *imperium*, the triumph had a marked sacral aspect,[30] and it thus imposes a consideration of the role of both religion and military glory in politics. On the whole, religion provided opportunities for political manipulation by those already in authority and the discussion may be postponed, but military glory was an undoubted factor in achieving leadership, our immediate concern.

The assessment is not easy. We are considering commanders, not infantrymen or non-commissioned officers, and the triumphal claims of generals throughout history are notoriously slippery, even those that are publicly accepted. Secondly, our sources are still more unreliable than usual in this area: accounts of the earlier years of famous men are too often fictions or semi-fictions supplied *post factum* because they are appropriate to men who have acquired fame. Nevertheless the fictions are significant as a type: they unanimously point to the indispensability of a proper military career and if possible of a family tradition of military achievement. The example of the elder Cato is sufficient.[31] 'In the whole of antiquity', it has been said 'there is not a single general who . . . did not feel it necessary, at least on occasion, to demonstrate his personal qualities by some prestigious action.'[32] Be that as it may, the most severe sceptic cannot deny that the command structure

[28] See E. S. Staveley, 'The *Fasces* and *Imperium Maius*', *Historia* 12 (1963) 458–64; B. Gladigow, 'Die sakralen Funktionen der Liktoren', in *Aufstieg und Niedergang der römischen Welt* ed. H. Temporini 1 2 (1972), pp. 295–314; Mommsen (1887–8) 1 373–93.

[29] See J. S. Richardson, 'The Triumph, the Praetors and the Senate in the Early Second Century B.C.', *Journal of Roman Studies* 65 (1975) 50–63, covering a wider time-span than the title suggests.

[30] H. S. Versnel, *Triumphus* (Leiden 1970).

[31] Astin (1978) ch. 1–2, who is ready to believe the claims.

[32] Garlan (1975) 148; cf. Harris (1979) 38–40.

within Greek and Roman armies was a monopoly of the upper classes, and that individual members of the ruling families had no choice in the matter: unlike politics, military command was not escapable (until the first century B.C.) at least at the 'brigade' level. Nor did all but the poorest citizens have any choice: Socrates fought in battle as a hoplite, at least twice when he was already in his forties.

There is nothing in modern experience quite like this. War was a normal part of life; not all periods compared in intensity with the Persian and Peloponnesian wars or with the Hannibalic War, but hardly a year went by without requiring a formal decision to fight, followed by a muster and the necessary preparations, and finally combat at some level. The majority of the citizens who participated directly in this decision-making had already had personal experience of war and could reasonably expect to be called upon again. The army was a citizen militia in the strict sense: there was no military class, no proper officer caste distinct from the social hierarchy in its civilian aspect. The requirement that political leaders shall have had, and continue to demonstrate, military distinction was therefore serious and comprehensible.

The nuances in individual cases elude us, to be sure. We really cannot know whether Aristides or Pericles or the elder Cato was competent as a general, let alone distinguished; why the two Athenians who appear to have been their ablest military leaders in the Peloponnesian War, Lamachus and Demosthenes, seem to have had no interest in politics; whether some Romans with distinguished military records sought the consulship solely as an honour without any genuinely *political* ambition. Nor are we in a position to assess the contempt and disgust with which Thucydides (4.27–37) narrates in detail how Cleon in 425 B.C. boastfully promised to regain Pylos within twenty days and proceeded to do just that. Yet even that story, whatever the truth about Cleon's personality or military capacity, well illustrates the pattern.

And again important differences are to be noted between Greece – that is to say, Athens – and Rome. In classical Athens, there was no automatic tie between any of the traditional magistracies (such as archons) and high military command. The *strategoi* were most untypical: they were elected, not chosen by lot, and they were eligible for reelection, obviously because known military skill was thought to be a necessary condition. Yet, the incomplete evidence also suggests that in fact they were of three recognizably distinct types, those like Cimon or Alcibiades, both militarily skilled and politically ambitious, men like Lamachus and Demosthenes who were chosen solely because of their known military ability, and others like Pericles and Cleon selected because they were ranking political leaders (though they were also expected to lead armies). In republican Rome, in contrast, military command remained both a duty and a prerogative of the two consuls, and was no doubt often enough the main reason why an individual sought the office. Strict adherence to the rules also created the paradox that Rome, the conquest-state, not infrequently suffered from incompetent commanders until their year's term of office expired. Only when more than two generals were needed simultaneously did Rome turn to others, and even then the original principle was preserved by bringing in praetors, and then by proroguing consuls and praetors for military purposes as proconsuls and propraetors.[33]

Obviously the quality of the relationship between civilian and military activity coloured political life and was in turn affected by the latter. Thus, in fourth-century Athens an important change set in, as I indicated earlier. Despite the continued warfare, there was a growing divorce between political and military leadership. This development was noticed and accented by contemporary writers, especially by critics of the system. Yet it appears not to have weakened the standing of the main politicians (who continued to serve as hoplites and, if rich enough, as trierarchs in the navy). The considerable increase in professionalism on the military side no doubt contributed but I cannot believe that it was a sufficient explanation. Rome's armies were, if anything, more professional but no comparable change occurred there. What happened in Rome in the final century of the Republic was different and in the end shattering. Whereas the Athenian state, and that means the *demos*, retained control over the professional generals, so that neither Conon nor Iphicrates played a serious political role,[34] the Roman Republic was ultimately destroyed by a series of very political commanders, from Marius to Julius Caesar, who were not subject to comparable popular control.

[33] This very brief account is necessarily oversimplified. I have, for example, ignored the early Roman dictator, an official with superior powers, normally military, appointed in a crisis for a period not exceeding six months.
[34] Pritchett (1971–9) II ch. 2–3.

Several centuries had elapsed by then, and none of the behaviour patterns or developments I have sketched are intelligible without an understanding of the politics involved. Neither élite allies and competitors nor the populace were passive bystanders. They had to be appealed to, consulted, manipulated, manoeuvred and outmanoeuvred; in sum, involved politically in different ways. That was the price paid for the city-state system with its element of popular participation.

4

POPULAR PARTICIPATION

A people is not just a political entity, as was once hoped. Parties, organized campaigns, and leaders make up the reality, if not the promise, of electoral regimes . . . Elections are rituals in function and in form, and the choice of parts is fairly limited. The pretensions therefore are standardized, and the conventions of expressing them are equally predictable. The voters' expectations are not, as a rule, particularly great, and their tolerance for eccentricities and departures from the script is low.[1]

That quotation from Judith Shklar, chosen almost at random, represents a common evaluation of contemporary democracy, though with the overtones of what its critics have come to call the élitist school. I began with it not because I am here concerned either with its descriptive accuracy or with the élitist arguments approving public apathy – I have discussed that elsewhere[2] – but because a preliminary warning seems essential. The equation, democracy = electoral regime, is so strongly entrenched in our culture that a conscious effort to put it wholly aside is required in the study of ancient politics. 'Electoral regime' is a completely wrong label for Greece, an inadequate one for Rome. There *were* elections, and they had their element of ritual, their pretensions and conventions, their apathetic voters. But there were also assemblies with the (at least formal) power of final decision on issues. There was, in short, a measure of genuine popular *participation*. There was also leadership drawn almost exclusively from élite strata, and the complicated and changing relationships between leaders and *demos* merit detailed consideration,[3] looking at Athens and Rome in turn rather than in tandem. As always, we shall restrict ourselves to the periods I have defined earlier, and we have to bear in mind that, though

---

[1] J. Shklar, 'Let Us Not Be Hypocritical', *Daedalus* 108 no. 3 (1979) 1–25, at pp. 14–15.

[2] Finley (1973*b*); cf. Q. Skinner, 'The Empirical Theorists of Democracy: A Plague on Both Their Houses', *Political Theory* 1 (1973) 287–306.

[3] It surely does not require argument to reject the view (e.g. of Kluwe (1976), (1977)) that popular participation is reduced to a charade by the fact that leadership was monopolized by the élite; see, e.g., Meier (1980) 260–5.

Athens was an exceptional city-state, there are hints – no more can be claimed – that in general terms political behaviour was similar in other *poleis* of some size with systems that the Greeks called democratic.

Athenian citizenship was normally acquired by birth only; it was rarely granted to others and then only by a formal vote of the Assembly, the ultimate governmental authority. Meetings of the Assembly were open to every citizen who chose to attend. There he had a direct vote on proposals, which were openly debated, amended if desired, and sometimes initiated; and he voted openly before his fellow citizens. In principle the powers of the Assembly were boundless:[4] for a fleeting period in 411 B.C. it even abolished itself and replaced democracy by an oligarchy. There were two councils. The Council of the Areopagus, an archaic survival composed of ex-archons with life membership, was reduced to a shadowy existence in 462 B.C. because all the important conciliar functions were thereafter in the hands of the Council of 500 (to whom the single word 'Council' will be restricted).[5] They were selected by lot from all citizens over the age of thirty who chose to allow their names to go forward, with a compulsory geographical spread. Their term of office was one year and a man could serve only twice in his lifetime.[6]

Nearly all the officials were also selected by lot – the hallmark of democracy for the Greeks (Aristotle, *Rhetoric* 1365b30–31) – and they were restricted to a single year in office, not renewable.[7] Their qualifications (more precisely, their worthiness) could be chal-

---

[4] This generalization is not substantially weakened by the relatively rare fourth-century practice known as *nomothesia*, on which see now two articles by M. H. Hansen, in *Greek, Roman and Byzantine Studies* 19 (1978) 315–30; 20 (1979) 27–53; with further discussion in *Classica et Mediaevalia* 32 (1971–80) 87–104, the fullest available examination of the evidence, though, in my judgment, with too mechanical and formal a distinction between *nomos* and *psephisma*, conventionally translated 'law' and 'decree', respectively. The technical changes introduced into the machinery of Athenian government in the fourth century are well summarized by P. J. Rhodes, 'Athenian Democracy after 403 B.C.', *Classical Journal* 75 (1979/80) 305–23.

[5] The revival of the Areopagus, which in the Hellenistic period became (and remained under Roman rule) the effective government in Athens, is a neat symbol of the destruction of Athenian democracy.

[6] See Rhodes (1972), esp. 179–207.

[7] The exceptions to selection by lot were the *strategoi*, possibly the highest financial officers, and such *ad hoc* posts as ambassadors. The best account remains that of Headlam (1933).

lenged beforehand by formal procedures open to every citizen, and they had to submit to an account of stewardship at the end of their term.[8] Such controls, entailing the risk of heavy penalties, clearly weakened the power of officials with respect to the Assembly and the courts. So did the extensive fragmentation of offices and duties and also the absence of a hierarchical service within which an individual was expected to proceed *by election* in an orderly sequence (such as the Roman *cursus honorum*). Although property qualifications survived for a few posts *de iure*, they were in most cases eventually allowed to disappear *de facto* (Aristotle, *Constitution of Athens* 47.1). Most court cases, finally, were in the hands of bodies (usually large) open to all citizens: the Assembly, the Council, and the 'juries' in the heliastic courts. The latter, chosen by lot from a roster of 6,000 volunteers, received a *per diem* allowance while serving; so did Council members, probably some officials (though there is unclarity about them), soldiers and sailors, and in the fourth century also those who attended meetings of the Assembly.[9]

On paper all this adds up to widespread participation in governmental affairs. What was the reality about the extent or degree of political activity, understanding and interest? That there were a substantial number of apathetic citizens may be taken for granted, but we cannot put a figure to them. One common approach is to pretend to statistical 'objectivity' by making disparaging remarks about the numbers who actually attended meetings of the Assembly and to back them by purely hypothetical statements (disguised as facts) about the behaviour of the peasant majority of the population, their lack of culture and education, their unconcern with anything other than the hard struggle for existence, their inability to take the time for a journey into the city on meeting-days. Further support is claimed from passages in the poets and Plato that glorify the man who 'minds his own business', who does not meddle in

---

[8] E. Hoyer, *Die Verantwortlichkeit und Rechenschaftspflicht der Behörden in Griechenland* (Karlsbad 1928); M. Piérart, 'Les *euthynoi* athéniens', *L'Antiquité classique* 40 (1971) 526–73.

[9] See now M. H. Hansen, '*Misthos* for Magistrates in Classical Athens', *Symbolae Osloenses* 54 (1979) 5–22, though not all his conclusions are persuasive; also his 'Seven Hundred *Archai* in classical Athens', *Greek, Roman and Byzantine Studies* 21 (1980) 151–73.

public affairs.[10] Pericles in the Funeral Oration dismissed such men as 'useless' (Thucydides 2.40.2), but that, we are assured, was mere wartime rhetoric.[11] None of this will do. 'An aura of fraudulence', writes Adkins with full justification, 'hangs about such imputations in the works of the *agathoi* writers who are our sources', men, 'who "know" themselves to be socially superior, and "know" that they have a right to be politically superior, but nevertheless find themselves at a serious disadvantage in the existing political situation'.[12] That situation was created by the right of socially inferior citizens to participate directly, in the Assembly, in the decisions on all public matters. If upper-class expressions of disapproval have any evidentiary value about the practice, they surely argue for, not against, widespread participation.

The Assembly was not a parliament with a fixed membership; no doubt fewer ordinary citizens took the trouble to attend routine sessions but it is unimaginable that the question of whether or not to go to war with Sparta met with similar disinterest. Even peasants, the most underemployed occupational group in any society, could take the time off; so could self-employed artisans and shopkeepers in the city. In Aristotle's day, the Assembly normally met on forty days evenly spaced throughout the year, perhaps less often in the fifth century – not a large inroad into anyone's time, especially as meetings often lasted less than a full day and never more.[13]

The best analysis of the evidence, some of it archaeological, suggests that attendance ran to 6,000 in the fifth century, to substantially more in the fourth.[14] How does one assess the significance of such Assembly figures, when the number of eligible men reached a peak of perhaps 40,000 in 431 B.C., declining thereafter to 25,000 or so? Any answer will be subjective, but there is

---

[10] See V. Ehrenberg, 'Polypragmosyne: a Study in Greek Politics', *Journal of Hellenic Studies* 67 (1947) 46–67, reprinted in Ehrenberg (1965) 466–501; Grossmann (1950) 126–37.

[11] For our purposes it does not matter whether any or all of the Funeral Oration accurately reflects Pericles' wording or views. See generally H. Strasburger, 'Thukydides und die politische Selbstdarstellung der Athener', in Strasburger (1982) II 676–708, originally published in *Hermes* 86 (1958).

[12] A. W. Adkins, '*Polupragmosune* and "Minding One's Own Business" . . .', *Classical Philology* 71 (1976) 301–27, at pp. 318, 325.

[13] M. H. Hansen, 'The Duration of a Meeting of the Athenian Ecclesia', *Classical Philology* 74 (1979) 43–9.

[14] M. H. Hansen, 'How Many Athenians Attended the Ecclesia?', *Greek, Roman and Byzantine Studies* 17 (1976) 115–34.

perhaps a better approach to the problem of participation through the Council. Its 500 members were selected by lot, on a system by which each of the demes (or parishes) of Attica, *including the rural demes*, was represented in proportion to its population, and by which no man could serve before the age of thirty and then only twice in his lifetime. The names of more than 3,000 Council members are now known and fewer than 3 per cent of them can be identified as having had a second term.[15] Even very small demes seem normally to have been able to supply their quotas. The quantitative range in deme membership was very great and no attempt was ever made to bring about more equal ratios. Nor did deme membership necessarily imply deme residence: the former was inherited generation after generation regardless of any changes in domicile, so that membership of rural demes became increasingly an absentee one with the slow but steady movement from country to city. All this, together with selection by lot and restricted tenure, undermines the persistent modern error of considering the Council as a representative body in the only meaningful sense of that term.[16] The Athenians were following the principle of rotation, not of representation, thereby further strengthening the direct democracy of the Assembly.[17]

In any decade, something between a fourth and a third of the total citizenry over thirty would have been Council members, serving daily (in principle) throughout the year and for a tenth of that year on full duty as so-called *prytaneis*.[18] Given the range and importance of Council business, Lotze is therefore justified in calling the Council 'a school of democracy'.[19] Then one must add the thousands who had court experience, not rarely judging political cases; the hundreds of officials, from market wardens to archons, each selected by lot and restricted to a single, unrepeatable tenure of one year; and the men who had served abroad in the army and the navy. These experienced men, it must not be forgotten, were free to attend Assembly meetings at any time, whether in or out of office.

[15] See Rhodes (1980) 192–3, with lists on pp. 197–201, supplemented in *Zeitschrift für Papyrologie und Epigraphik* 41 (1981) 101–2.

[16] This error runs through Traill (1975) from the opening page; behind him stands J. A. O. Larsen, *Representative Government in Greek and Roman History* (Berkeley 1955), ch. 1.

[17] Weber (1972) 666.　　[18] See Rhodes (1972) ch. 1.

[19] D. Lotze, 'Entwicklungslinien der athenischen Demokratie im 5. Jh. v. Chr.', *Oikumene* 4 (1983) 9–24, at p. 20.

At least half the Athenian multitude deciding from ignorance on matters of state, a favourite target of Thucydides and Plato and many modern historians, thus melts away on close examination.[20] But how fair a sample of the total citizenry was even this large sample? That is an important question we can answer only by guesses.[21] It seems reasonable to think that under normal conditions Assembly attendance was weighted in favour of the more aged and the urban citizens, though the degree of weighting is beyond even guessing. But what were normal conditions? There were easily recognized abnormal circumstances and abnormal issues. The former included such contingencies as the absence of a large number of hoplites on an expedition (or, on another social level, of a large number of seamen) or the presence in the city of a large peasant element when an enemy army invaded the countryside, as occurred several times during the Peloponnesian War, permanently in the final decade. Abnormal issues included, above all, proposals for major constitutional change or decisions whether or not to engage in a major war, both questions that immediately and directly affected the lives of many who sat in the Assembly on the day and cast the votes that would decide. For Aristotle, that was the key to the qualitative difference to be found between political and forensic oratory (*Rhetoric* 1354b22-55a2).

Our guessing-games are an academic exercise; not so for the political leaders of the time, who not only would have had a fair idea beforehand of the probable composition and calculated accordingly but would have taken such steps as lay in their power to affect that composition by bringing out the vote. To appreciate how much that mattered to them, we must concentrate our minds and our imaginations on a political system without modern parallels: there were no structured political parties and there was no government in the sense of an appointed or elected group of men formally entrusted for the moment with the right or the duty to make policy proposals to the Assembly, which had the more or less unrestricted power of making binding decisions. To be sure, when the Assembly met soon after dawn, it often had before it a proposal, drafted by

---

[20] See generally A. G. Woodhead, '*Isegoria* and the Council of 500', *Historia* 16 (1967) 129-40.

[21] For what follows I draw on Finley (1962) and I shall not bother to indicate changes in stress or nuance.

the Council. However, that annually replaced body of 500 men selected by lot, occupied though it was with the whole range of administration as well as with preparing legislation, was not a 'government' in our sense. Nor was there an official opposition. Alternative policies were formulated within a small political class for which there was no technical term because it had no structured existence. It was up to them to steer their proposals through the Council and the Assembly, and in the end the latter was free to approve, amend or reject any recommendation, from whatever source it emanated.[22] A mass meeting of several thousand men who chose to be present on that occasion listened to speakers – to men who opted to take the floor, without holding any office, without any formal duty or obligation – and then voted by show of hands,[23] all in one day or less than a day. On controversial matters the debates were 'real': there were no formal party line-ups, no whips, no machinery to predetermine the final vote irrespective of the speechmaking. It was in those debates that leadership was tested, that politics were made and unmade, and only the naive or innocent observer can believe that a Pericles came to a vital Assembly meeting armed with nothing but his intelligence, his knowledge, his charisma and his oratorical skill, essential as all four attributes were.

The range of requisite knowledge was considerable, as Socrates had suggested to Glaucon; in the absence of a bureaucracy or a party, direct personal participation was necessary all the time (with a qualification I shall soon come to); the pattern of Assembly meetings at short intervals all the year round left no respite, no breathing-space such as a parliamentary recess. A single text will help to illustrate, a long though incomplete inscription of 425 or 424 B.C. introducing a radically increased assessment of the tribute paid annually by the subject-states in the Athenian empire. It is a technical document, detailing the procedures to be followed and the penalties for violation. There is no preamble, no explanation or justification of the measure, and since Thucydides failed to mention the reassessment – perhaps his most famous 'silence' – scholars have had a field day over the precise chronology, the context and the

---

22 The evidence for the relationship between Council and Assembly, considerable but far from straightforward, is fully analysed by Rhodes (1972) ch. 2; see his ch. 3 on the administrative role of the Council.
23 See M. H. Hansen, 'How Did the Athenian *Ecclesia* Vote?', *Greek, Roman and Byzantine Studies* 18 (1977) 123–37.

motives.[24] None of that interests me now, but several simple facts, not in the least controversial, command our attention.

The inscription records the decision of the Assembly following a proposal by the Council and, as an appendix, the new assessment, city by city, subsequently fixed by the 'assessors' chosen in accordance with the decree. Although commentators with a nose for such things have detected that 'the sequence of clauses is extremely unsystematic' and have therefore surmised that 'the text was drafted by an inexperienced man',[25] even they must concede that exact knowledge of the tribute system underlay its preparation. The man who presented the proposal to the Assembly (whether he was its drafter or not) was named Thoudippos. He is otherwise unattested in Athenian political life, though there is a considerable probability that he was the son-in-law of Cleon and a man of property (whose descendants were involved in a squalid dispute over an inheritance).[26]

Cleon was the most powerful figure in Athens when the tribute reassessment decree was passed. We do not *know* – that is, no one tells us – that he had anything to do with the decree. Nor do we know how much debate there was in the Assembly about it, or whether Cleon took the floor himself. Let us nevertheless make the reasonable assumption that he was the policy-maker behind the re-assessment. How would he, or anyone else in his position, have gone about it? It would have been physically impossible for him to collect the data personally because there were too many matters of state business to permit one man to control the detailed information. As there was no bureaucratic apparatus to do the work for him, his only recourse was to an unofficial, unpaid entourage, among whom there was a rough division of labour.[27] Even from the

[24] See the commentary in Meiggs/Lewis (1969) no. 69, with bibliography.
[25] Meiggs/Lewis (1969) p. 197.   [26] Davies (1971) no. 7252.
[27] My immediate concern is with those experts whom I believe to have been indispensable in the entourage of political leaders; cf. Connor (1971) 124–7, who is interested in the leaders themselves. This is one, though by no means the only, context in which to assume activity by the 'clubs' (*hetaireiai*) about which we hear so much but so little in concrete detail; see G. M. Calhoun, *Athenian Clubs in Politics and Litigation* (Univ. of Texas, 1913). Because the evidence is concentrated on the mutilation of the herms in 415 and the oligarchic coup of 411 B.C., modern writers are obsessed with the conspiratorial role of some clubs and overlook the routine day-to-day activity which was essential under prevailing political conditions. Administrators as such also required experts, of course: A. Andrewes, 'The Mytilene Debate: Thucydides 3.36–49', *Phoenix* 16 (1962) 64–85, at pp. 83–4.

scrappy epigraphical remains and the rare references in the literature it can be seen that there were identifiable experts, specialists in international affairs, finances and so on. In the re-assessment case, Thoudippos happened to have been a member of the Council but that was not a necessary condition: there were simple procedures by which a non-member could approach the Council or be called in by them. But, if he or Cleon standing behind him wished the proposal to become law, one of them or a known associate had to take the floor in the Assembly.

Now let us pursue our imaginative reconstruction from the other side, that of the X thousand men who attended the Assembly meeting. If there was disagreement in principle about the vast increase in tribute being proposed – and I repeat that we are completely in the dark about this – that would have been debated (or it might already have been argued out in general terms at an earlier meeting). It is inconceivable, however, that much of the detail of the decree we possess could have been discussed at this stage, in an open-air mass meeting. They would have been accepted on faith, that is to say, from confidence in the sponsors of the measure and the Council which had formulated it. Critics, if there were any, would have been constrained to attack the principle or the sponsors; no one could have followed arguments about the details. Therefore, when I spoke of 'identifiable experts' and 'known associates' I had in mind not men whom modern historians can identify but those whose expertise and connections were recognized by the members of the relevant Assembly.

I shall illustrate further by quoting at some length, though I have reluctantly deleted much of the rhetoric, Demosthenes' account delivered in a speech (18.169–79) nine years after the dramatic situation late in 339 B.C. when the news reached Athens that Philip of Macedon had seized Elatea on the north-western border of Boeotia:

It was evening you remember. Suddenly news was brought to the *prytaneis* of the capture of Elatea. At this they got up in the middle of dinner, and started at once to drive people away from the stalls in the market . . . Others proposed to summon the *strategoi* and called for the herald. The city was in an uproar. At dawn the next day the *prytaneis* summoned the Council to the chamber, and you [the citizens] moved into the Assembly, where, before the Council could conclude their business and prepare a proposal, the whole *demos* were already seated. The Council appeared, announced the news they had received, and brought the messenger forward to repeat it. The herald then voiced the question, 'Who desires to speak?' No one moved. The question was repeated several times without a man standing up . . . It appeared that that moment and occasion demanded not merely patriotic feeling . . . but familiarity with public affairs from the beginning and a right judgment of Philip's aims and motives . . . I therefore was the man who showed such capacity that day. I came forward and addressed the Assembly . . . There was universal applause, not a sound of dissent. And I did not speak without proposing a motion.[28]

A splendid *ex parte* statement, of course, but in outline certainly correct. After some years of vacillation and disagreement about the right line to pursue against Philip, Demosthenes was on that morning able to win overwhelming support for his motion that Athens should negotiate a military alliance with Thebes on terms substantially different from any previous proposal. An examination of his earlier speeches on the subject confirms his words: political leaders spoke on the assumption that the Assembly expected to rely on their information and their judgment, and then to choose between alternative proposals or policies on the basis of the facts and the arguments they had heard.[29] How did one attain such standing (or lose it)? Although the Assembly gave the final answer, it is inconceivable that the determination of Athenian policy over two or more centuries of considerable stability was turned into nothing more than a continuous contest in oratorical skill. Demosthenes was no less able an orator on the occasions when he failed to persuade the Assembly than in the moments of success. Besides, dominant political leaders did not necessarily address the Assembly themselves on all occasions: they often relied on their identifiable expert-lieutenants.[30] The sources are misleading on this score: so much of the bulk consists either of actual orations, edited for publication, or of literary speeches that fill the pages of the historians in a tradition that had its roots in the Homeric poems.

[28] Translated by A. N. W. Saunders, in the Penguin Classics volume, *Demosthenes and Aeschines* (with a few slight modifications). See Aeschines 2.67–8 for another reference to Demosthenes' appearance in the Assembly with the handwritten text of a proposed decree.

[29] Correctly Starr (1974) 35–6. His concluding rhetorical question, 'Is this situation really very different in modern states?', should be answered in the affirmative: no modern *demos* votes directly on such policy questions.

[30] That is the qualification I mentioned earlier to the proposition that leadership required direct personal participation all the time.

Otherwise the sources concern themselves with alliances and conflicts within the political class,[31] or they play variations on the theme of moral condemnation, succinctly expressed by Thucydides (2.65.10): Pericles' 'successors were more equal to each other, and each seeking to become the first man they even offered the conduct of affairs to the whims of the people'.

For many years the activities of Philip of Macedon had been the central problem in Athenian foreign policy. What kind and how much of a threat was he to Athens? It is enough to look at the short period from the so-called Peace of Philocrates in 346 to Elatea seven years later (about a year after a formal declaration of war between Philip and Athens).[32] Even a full-time professional politician such as Demosthenes must have found it difficult to keep in touch with diplomatic and military activity involving dozens of independent Greek *poleis*, Macedonia, Thrace, the Persian Empire and Egypt. Nowhere, furthermore, is there better evidence of the central role of personal associates and lieutenants in Greek politics.

Now Philip's capture of Elatea settled the matter. As we have seen, among the people who filled the Assembly by dawn on the day following arrival of the news from Elatea were a considerable number with direct experience in office, in the Council, in the courts, and in previous sessions of the Assembly, at many of which the problem of Philip of Macedon had been vigorously argued. They did not come with empty heads or 'open minds', and they knew that for many of them the day's decision would mean immediate army service and probably combat. That knowledge would have focused the minds sharply; it would have given the debate a reality and spontaneity that modern parliaments may once have had but now notoriously lack.[33] If this time, untypically and

---

[31] Modern historians are often happy to follow (and even outdo) them in this concern: see the criticism of Connor (1971) by C. Ampolo, in *Archeologia classica* 27 (1975) 95-100.

[32] See G. L. Cawkwell, 'Demosthenes' Policy after the Peace of Philocrates', *Classical Quarterly*, n.s. 13 (1963) 120-38, 200-13, reprinted in *Philip and Athens*, ed. S. Perlman (Cambridge and New York 1973), ch. 10. The most detailed account is that of F. R. Wüst, *Philipp II von Makedonien und Griechenland in den Jahren von 346 bis 338* (Munich 1938).

[33] I more or less repeat what I wrote at somewhat greater length in Finley (1973b) 20-3. I owe the notion of the 'spontaneity' of such debates to O. Reverdin, 'Remarques sur la vie politique d'Athènes au Ve siècle', *Museum Helveticum* 2 (1945) 201-12.

somewhat surprisingly, there was in fact no debate (we may ignore Demosthenes' coquetry in holding back at first), then we have the right to conclude, first, that minds had been sufficiently made up; secondly, that it was generally expected that Demosthenes would (and should) indicate the steps to be taken. And he had come prepared, with the text of a formal decree in his hand, as he would come prepared at the subsequent assemblies that would decide on the financial, diplomatic and military consequences of his initial proposal.

Presumably the messenger who brought the news from Elatea was more or less official and trustworthy, unlike the orator's private informant on another occasion, who, he assured the Assembly without identifying him, was 'a man incapable of lying' (2.17). There is no suggestion in Demosthenes' account that anyone doubted the Elatean report, as was often the case (e.g. Thucydides 8.1.1). Reliability of information from abroad was a chronically serious problem; so was delay, whereas internal dissemination was extremely rapid except when secrecy was involved.[34] That was the reality of a face-to-face society depending on the spoken, not the written, word. Some twelve hours elapsed between the arrival of the messenger from Elatea and the moment when Demosthenes rose to speak in the Assembly; twelve hours of 'uproar', Demosthenes said nine years later, but are we to imagine that his supporters and many others were not busy preparing and organizing, or at least talking seriously? There was even enough time in which to spread the news to, and bring in citizens from, the countryside, though not from the most distant demes.

I asked, not for the first time, what we are to *imagine* because on this central aspect of politics we have only the vaguest and most indirect clues. The reliance of the average citizen on verbal reports cannot be exaggerated, not only for the results of battles and other events abroad but equally for ordinary internal matters, such as the state of the treasury, the money needed for a campaign or a major public-works programme, previous legislation relevant to a current proposal, terms of past treaties, available military manpower, the performance of individual officials, and so on through the whole

---

[34] The basic study is the massive and sophisticated book by Riepl (1913); though almost entirely devoted to Rome, much is equally applicable to Greece *mutatis mutandis*; Starr (1974) is concerned solely with foreign affairs.

gamut of public business. Much was available in writing; there were public archives of a sort and the Athenian state (unlike many others) also filled the public areas with an extraordinary collection of notices, often inscribed on stone or bronze, including tribute lists, decrees, treaties and public accounts. The political experts consulted documents, as cross-references in decrees and treaties show,[35] and so did administrative officials. But no one else did – on all occasions at which documents were referred to, whether Assembly meetings or court cases, they were read out by the clerk, and, as the vote was taken immediately upon conclusion of the verbal proceedings, there was no opportunity to check facts or even to discuss contradictory statements of fact. No doubt any citizen was free to go to the archives or wander about the streets reading inscriptions beforehand, but only the most eccentric would have done so. It is symptomatic that not even Thucydides bothered except rarely and for special reasons.

This was not only a face-to-face society, it was also a Mediterranean society in which people congregated out of doors, on market-days, on numerous festive occasions, and all the time in the harbour and the town square. Citizens were members of varied formal and informal groups – the family and household, the neighbourhood or village, military and naval units, occupational groups (farmers at harvest-time or urban crafts which tended to concentrate in particular streets), upper-class dining-clubs, innumerable private cult-associations. All provided opportunities for news and gossip, for discussion and debate, for the continuing political education I stressed earlier. Nor was this an exclusively urban phenomenon. Athenian peasants lived not on isolated farm homesteads but in hamlets and villages, with their village squares, local cult-centres and occasional assemblies, with a political life of their own that was linked constitutionally with that of the city-state: the demes (parishes) registered citizens and kept the rosters, and they provided the lists from which members of the Council and many officials were chosen annually by lot.[36] Aristophanic jokes about rude and ignorant rustics should not be turned into a generalization. One of

---

[35] E.g. Meiggs/Lewis (1969) no. 31, a decree regulating relations with Phaselis, lines 8–11: 'The case shall be tried in Athens, in the polemarch's court, just as for the Chians.'

[36] The only full-scale study is the still valuable one of Haussoullier (1883), though I believe he underestimates the extent of popular participation in deme political life.

Theophrastus' jibes (*Characters* 4.6) is that the rustic inappropriately reports assembly business in detail to his farm labourers.

As there were multiple forums for political discussion and education, it must follow that they were utilized by men of political ambition (and their supporters) in order to advance themselves and their policies. Canvassing and lobbying were surely continuous and unremitting, of a kind that we are unfamiliar with precisely because it was directed ultimately to actual decision-making rather than to the election of representatives who would have the power of decision. All this is unfortunately taken for granted by contemporary writers to the point of total silence. Instead they consider two other aspects of political behaviour. One is the image-building of the leaders, through their military record, real or not, which we have already considered; through their oratorical skills, obviously important when the popular Assembly occupied the central role; and through their munificence, both on city-wide projects and locally, in the demes and villages.

Financial outlay had two faces in this context. This was a world in which wealth was unequivocally admired and boasted about;[37] in which both public and private munificence were quickly and widely known, a never-ending theme not only among commentators but also among the benefactors themselves (as the surviving orations reveal in ways that modern readers tend to find distasteful). But munificence easily invokes accusations of corruption, and this is the other aspect of political life that occupies much attention among ancient writers. Charges of disreputable private behaviour, lying and corruption in public affairs are stereotypes: one need only read the speeches of Aeschines and Demosthenes directed against each other. Such accusations are wholly beyond our control: we can say no more than that they cannot be either *all* true or *all* unfounded. Given that it is certain, for instance, that the kings of Persia and Macedon were prepared to dispense gold liberally in advancing their interests in Greece, it is equally certain that some Greek political leaders accepted the offer, but I know no way to determine the truth or falsity of such a charge against, say, Demosthenes, other than by an unacceptably subjective judgment about his 'morality' (in modern terms). Internal bribery, payment to individual citizens in return for their votes, is something else again, and about this sort

[37] See Finley (1973*a*) 35–41.

of charge I am sceptical. I cannot envisage how one proceeded, or could afford, to bribe jurors whose numbers could run to 1,000 and who were chosen by lot from a panel of 6,000 just as a trial was to begin, or citizens who attended the Assembly by the thousands.

Before turning from Athens to Rome I should say explicitly that I have been trying to describe Athenian political behaviour, not to judge it, whether from an absolute moral standpoint or from a contemporary view of social justice. I have in the past been found 'guilty of a certain romanticizing of Athenian government' and of misusing the term 'democracy' because the *demos* was a narrow minority that excluded women, slaves and members of the subject-states in the fifth-century empire.[38] It does not seem to me that a structural historical analysis of Greek (or any other) politics *in their own terms* either warrants such criticism or requires a litany of explicit moral condemnation. It is easy to score points over a dead society, more difficult and more rewarding to examine what they were trying to do, how they went about it, the extent to which they succeeded or failed, and why. The two kinds of consideration cannot be conflated without the risk, indeed the probability, of getting them both wrong. In both Athens and Rome the citizen-bodies were minorities exploiting large numbers of men, free and slave. It still remains to explain why both were pragmatically successful and politically stable for long periods, why in both there was a constant tension between élite leaders and the populace, including the peasantry; yet why one retained and even enlarged popular participation, while the other persistently contained it within narrow limits. One may disapprove of either or both societies heartily: the problem of explanation does not disappear because of that.

Rome can now be examined more briefly by highlighting the most important differences from Athens. There is no need to repeat

[38] J. R. Fears, in a review of Finley (1973*b*) in *Annals of the Amer. Academy of Political and Social Science* 410 (1973) 197–8, and B. Hindess, reviewing both Finley (1973*a*) and (1973*b*) in *The Sociological Review* 23 (1975) 678–97, respectively. Hindess' notion that the Athenian empire was 'a larger political unit – a state' in which Athens was only one of many members (p. 681) simply baffles me by its incomprehension of ancient Greek institutions. So does the argument of R. A. Dahl that Athens was not an example of a participatory democracy because 'the demos consisted of all those who *were* qualified to govern': 'Procedural Democracy', in *Philosophy, Politics and Society*, 5th ser., ed. P. Laslett and J. Fishkin (Oxford 1974), p. 119.

what I have already said about a face-to-face Mediterranean society, an oral culture, the difficulties of obtaining and diffusing essential information, the interrelationship between domestic and foreign/ military affairs, the lack of separation between civilian and military leaders, the role of military glory, public munificence and patronage in obtaining and holding political leadership. Several important differences in these respects have already been noticed. Here I single out differences in scale, which in the course of time became so great as to heighten significantly the existing structural differences in political life. Thus, by the middle of the third century B.C. there were formal divisions ('tribes') of the rural population situated as far south as Capua in the south and the Adriatic to the east.[39] Eventually they extended to Lake Como and Venetia. The implication of such distances for anyone wishing to vote or otherwise participate politically in the city of Rome requires no elaboration.

Structurally, or constitutionally if one prefers, there were fundamental differences at every key point. There was not one assembly but three, which every citizen was free to attend when he wished (barring the unimportant exclusion of the tiny minority of patricians from the *concilium plebis*). However, the formal devices designed to ensure tight élite control accumulated until they amounted to a veritable straitjacket. The details are bewildering and often uncertain for several reasons – the patchy source-material, the frequent modifications in the practice by enactment or custom, the exceptional instances (especially in the last century of the Republic). Nevertheless, an 'ideal-type' summary is sufficient for the present discussion.[40] To begin with, there were no fixed meeting-dates, not even for the annual consular elections: an assembly met only when convened for a specific purpose, whether an election or a 'legislative' proposal, by a higher magistrate within whose power it lay to do so. Such a summons could be invalidated in various ways, by unfavourable auspices (to be considered later in this chapter), for

---

[39] See Taylor (1960) ch. 5. It also appears that Italian peasants often lived in more dispersed and isolated habitations than their Athenian counterparts: P. D. A. Garnsey, 'Where Did Italian Peasants Live?', *Proceedings of the Cambridge Philological Society*, n.s. 25 (1979) 1–25. This is a subject requiring further investigation with particular concern for regional differences, rooted in the pre-Roman history of the various areas: see briefly E. Gabba and M. Pasquinucci, *Strutture agrarie e allevamento transumante nell' Italia romana (III–I sec. a.C.)* (Pisa 1979), pp. 21–6.

[40] Taylor (1966) is fundamental; see also Nicolet (1976) ch. 7; Staveley (1972) pt II.

example, or by a 'veto' interposed by another magistrate of high rank or by a tribune prior to the actual voting.[41] And when an assembly finally met, there was no discussion; there was only a vote to elect from the list presented by the summoning magistrate or to approve or reject the bill he had submitted beforehand. It was not even permitted to vote on more than one proposal at a single sitting. The final count of votes was then not by individuals but by groups, so constituted as to weight the votes in favour of the wealthier strata, in the *comitia centuriata* so blatantly as to discount the votes of the poorer classes altogether except when there was a serious split within the élite; and that was the assembly that elected consuls and praetors and had the sole right to declare war.[42]

Such a brief enumeration of rules does not exhaust the difficulties placed in the way of participation by citizens who lacked independent means, especially those who lived away from the city of Rome. The rule, normally enforced, was that three *nundinae* (the Roman market-days at eight-day intervals) had to elapse between the summons and the meeting of the assembly. The interval provided an opportunity for one or more *contiones*, public meetings at which the proposer and others *who were invited* discussed the proposal without such formalities as amendments or votes. The citizenry at large thus had more than three weeks' notice of a forthcoming election and a chance to hear members of the élite speak more or less formally about the issues. On the other hand, proper participation required repeated attendance (in obvious contrast to the procedure of the Athenian Assembly), without any guarantee that the particular piece of business would finally be brought to a conclusion on the appointed day: a veto or the declaration of unfavourable auspices could be injected up to the last moment. Stamina, leisure or patronage, and sustained interest were all necessary conditions for

---

[41] The tribunician veto provides a neat example of the way in which institutions can change their role and character radically: originally introduced in the archaic period as a protective device for plebeians against an abuse of magisterial power, the tribunes and their prerogative of intervention were transformed into a major weapon in the struggle for power within the ruling class, quite without reference to plebeians and their rights.

[42] Many wars were of course 'undeclared': they were endemic in considerable areas of Italy and in regions that had been prematurely claimed as provinces, and there the commanders in the field 'made war' as they thought fit, more often than not in pursuit of plunder; see J. W. Rich, *Declaring War in the Roman Republic* ... (Brussels 1976), with qualifications briefly stated by Harris (1979) 263.

staying the course. Informal discussion was of course always possible wherever people congregated, but even that was made more difficult for those living outside Rome by a law adopted perhaps in 286 B.C. prohibiting assemblies from meeting on the market-days (they were already taboo on festival days). The elder Pliny (*Natural History* 18.13) thought that the aim was to prevent an assembly from interfering with the important business of a weekly market, but a modern commentator has rightly suggested the reverse explanation, the desire to keep away from an assembly large numbers of rustics other than 'those whom the political leaders in Rome had summoned to the city to cast their votes'.[43]

Roman officials, unpaid, were elected by popular vote – there was no place for selection by lot in this system[44] – but both the candidates themselves and those who had the right to nominate them were restricted to the élite, and the voting was then by the group procedure. Each office was for a single one-year tenure (with complicated variations in the consulship), normally following a fixed sequence at intervals of a few years. The highest officials had powers incomparable with any in Athens, as I have indicated earlier in a brief account of *imperium*, a concept that cannot be translated into Greek. That is why Roman tombstones always list the offices held by the defunct, classical Greek tombstones never. One particular magisterial power is worth specifying here, that of the censors to allocate new citizens to tribes, commonly employed in order to maintain the weighting advantages within and between tribes (and sometimes in order not to register new citizens at all).[45] Such powers expose some of the reality beneath the Roman practice, so unlike the Greek, of 'generosity' in extending citizenship not only to manumitted slaves (who were then concentrated in the four

---

[43] Michels (1967) 105. The point was made briefly but clearly by Livy 7.15.12–13 in an anachronistic context.

[44] On the restricted use of the lot in Rome for other purposes, see briefly Staveley (1972) 230–2.

[45] See Taylor (1960) ch. 16, with undue caution; more sharply on the non-registration of new citizens, G. Tibiletti, 'The "Comitia" during the Decline of the Roman Republic', *Studia et documenta historiae et iuris* 25 (1959) 94–127. The censorship was, strictly speaking, not classified among the magistracies, with its odd term of office, its lack of *imperium* and its changing conditions; see briefly A. E. Astin, 'The Censorship of the Roman Republic: Frequency and Regularity', *Historia* 31 (1982) 174–87.

urban tribes) but increasingly (in different degrees) to Latins and finally to other Italians.[46]

On completion of their year in office, the higher magistrates could normally expect to enter the Senate. Down to the late fourth century B.C. they in fact did so for life, until the censors were given the power to review the Senate's membership quinquennially and that included the power to expel existing members.[47] The reviews were in fact surprisingly spasmodic, so that there were longish stretches of time during which the notional composition of 300 dropped significantly while men waited years for admission. The number who failed to be admitted or who were actually expelled (upon conviction for certain offences, for instance) was not large, but the very existence of this censorial power served to bring to heel the occasional deviant magistrate; it did not substantially alter the fact that the Senate was an almost closed super-élite body of life members. And the Senate was the Roman council. The Senate, not the assemblies, was the keystone of the structure, and that body may properly be called a government. Given the unending chain of restraints on every kind of popular participation, it was hardly ever possible to take any governmental action in Rome unless and until the Senate approved. Why it approved or rejected a proposal, it is important to stress, was much of the time a well kept secret.[48]

Two more points will conclude this brief comparative survey of the elements of the constitution. Down to the final century of the Republic the higher Roman magistrates were immune from any formal accounting of their stewardship, apart from the threat of subsequent court proceedings or of censorial disapprobation; even a financial accounting, Mommsen concluded, 'may have existed in theory but hardly makes an appearance in practice'.[49] The court, finally, which went through a series of structural changes in the course of the Republic, remained in effect solidly upper-class. Only for a few major crimes was there a partial exception (even on the traditional view): provided that the death penalty was not invoked, in which case jurisdiction was transferred to the *comitia centuriata*,

---

[46] Gauthier (1974); in detail, E. Szanto, *Das griechische Bürgerrecht* (Freiburg 1892; repr. New York 1979); A. N. Sherwin-White, *The Roman Citizenship* (2nd ed., Oxford 1973).

[47] Mommsen (1887–8) II 1, 418–24; cf. in massive detail P. Willems, *Le sénat de la République romaine* (2nd ed., 3 vols. in 2, Louvain 1883–5) vol. 1.

[48] On this commonly overlooked point, see Harris (1979) 5–7, 255.

[49] Mommsen (1887–8) I 699–702.

these cases came before the *comitia tributa* or *concilium plebis* for 'popular' trial – hence the term *iudicium populi*.[50] But even in that restricted category of judicial proceedings, in which the political element was frequently visible, all the magisterial controls over the *comitia* remained in force, including the right to veto. There was nothing really comparable to the popular juries of Athens.

How the Roman élite succeeded in constraining popular participation to this extent, despite the inclusion in the political community not only of citizen-born peasants and townsmen but also of emancipated slaves and other outsiders, is a long story that is intimately linked with the continuous history of conquest and territorial expansion. Much is known about the specific measures and the war-and-conquest background that brought about this situation from the beginning of the Republic, but hardly anything about the politics beyond abstract generalizations about patron–client relations and the like. The fictions of Plutarch's *Coriolanus* or the speeches in the accounts in Livy and Dionysius of Halicarnassus of the patrician–plebeian struggles of the fifth and fourth centuries B.C. have no standing. The politics can be studied only for the centuries during which the essentially oligarchical system I have summarized functioned more or less stably, and that is perhaps best done by keeping in mind the politics of classical Athens as a measuring-stick.

Our leading authority on the subject, Lily Ross Taylor, opens her book on Roman voting assemblies in this way: 'Voting was a major occupation of the citizens who lived in Republican Rome or were there when the assemblies met . . . There was hardly a season of the year when Rome was free both from voting assemblies and from the campaigns in preparation for voting on choice of magistrates, on approval of laws, or on accusations.'[51] The palette of that picture, and also the substance, as I shall argue, derive too much from Plutarch on the Gracchi or from the feverish tone of some of

---

[50] For a full conventional account, which I have deliberately adopted, see A. H. M. Jones, *The Criminal Courts of The Roman Republic and Principate* (Oxford 1972), ch. 1, where the radical new view of Roman criminal procedure put forward by W. Kunkel, *Untersuchungen zur Entwicklung des römischen Kriminalverfahrens in vorsullanischer Zeit* (Abh. der bayerischen Akad. d. Wiss., Phil.-hist. Klasse, n. F. 56, 1962), is simply dismissed. Kunkel argued that 'ordinary criminal cases were apparently never brought before an assembly' but only political acts (p. 130).

[51] Taylor (1966) 1.

Cicero's letters in the next century, concerned with manoeuvres within the élite and not with 'the citizens'. The accents are clearly wrong. In the first place, all the evidence regarding the space and time required indicates that no assembly or voting procedure could have coped with more than perhaps 10,000 men (at least before Augustus),[52] while the numbers of eligible citizens residing in Rome rose to six figures, in Italy to seven figures. Secondly, the number of non-resident citizens who were in Rome at the right time is too passive a formulation; it understates the essential point that, on important issues, rural voters were *brought* to Rome where their weight was out of proportion to their numbers, given the existence of thirty-one rural tribes as against only four urban tribes. Tiberius Gracchus, we are told (Appian, *Civil Wars* 1.14), was hampered in his attempt at reelection because his rural supporters could not leave the harvest. That he did not have agents trying to rally these voters is as inconceivable as that he alone of Roman politicians canvassed the rural tribes. Thirdly, Roman assemblies, unlike the Athenian, passed very few 'laws' throughout the history of the Republic, so that except in such times of crisis as the Gracchan decade 'laws' could not have been a 'major' (or even minor) 'occupation' of most citizens. For the two hundred years preceding the tribunate of Tiberius Gracchus fewer than two hundred are known, even by a passing reference, and that figure includes declarations of war and awards of a triumph to a victorious commander.[53] Having once declared war, it is worth stressing, neither the centuriate nor any other assembly had any further say in the conduct of that war, save for an exceptional instance; and not even then in the least like the Athenian Assembly which was in continuous control of wars as of all other public affairs.[54] Fourthly, it is hard to conceive of popular excitement over the election of aediles or quaestors.

---

[52] See the details in Staveley (1972) ch. 8–10; cf. Nicolet (1976) 333–80.

[53] The actual count (including *plebiscita*) is 193 in the lists in G. Rotondi, *Leges publicae populi romani* (Milan 1912; repr. Hildesheim 1966), including a number of proposals that were probably rejected and some wholly doubtful instances. A detailed, inordinately long and repetitive account will be found in J. Bleicken, *Lex Publica* (Berlin and New York 1975), who builds on a false dichotomy between *Rechtsordnung* and *soziale Ordnung*; see the review by C. Meier in *Zeitschrift der Savigny-Stiftung für Rechtsgeschichte, Romanistische Abteilung* 95 (1978) 378–90.

[54] Compare the epigraphical fragments of Assembly action pertaining to the Sicilian expedition, Meiggs/Lewis (1969) no. 78, with the *senatus consultum* of 214 B.C. reported by Livy 24.11.

The narrowness of the activities allowed to the assemblies cannot be overstressed, at least with respect to the citizenry at large. And when candidates or proposals to be voted on were selected and screened by the oligarchy alone, when elections to the consulship and praetorship and declarations of war were in the hands of an assembly, the *comitia centuriata*, in which it was very rare for the lower-class centuries even to be summoned to cast their votes,[55] it would not be far from the truth to say that the Roman *populus* exercised influence not through participation in the formal machinery of government, through its voting power, but by taking to the streets, by agitation, demonstrations and riots, and this long before the days of the gangs and private armies of the civil-war century. That, I believe, is what the annalistic tradition reflected in Livy and Dionysius of Halicarnassus implied when it retrospectively attributed all plebeian victories in the early Republic to public demonstrations, to riots and 'secessions'. This admittedly unorthodox conclusion can be illustrated from the very rare instances (within our period) when popular pressure is known to have succeeded in opposition to a senatorial proposal. On matters of war and peace and foreign relations, no case is known in which a decision to make war was successfully resisted by the people; formal war-votes may have come to an end by the mid-second century B.C. anyway, while the evidence in the few attested cases of popular pressure on the Senate to embark on a war does not permit close scrutiny of the methods employed.[56]

Two election disputes are at least suggestive. In 185 B.C. one of the candidates for a vacancy created by the death of a praetor was Q. Fulvius Flaccus. The latter, a member of the perennially officeholding Fulvian *gens*, whose father had been four times consul, was then an aedile and the tribunes protested that his candidacy for the praetorship was illegal. A series of manoeuvres and negotiations ensued, reported in some detail by Livy (39.39.1–10), but Fulvius refused to withdraw, the Senate finally decreed that because of his obstinacy and, in Livy's words, the perverse partiality of the people (*prava studia hominum*), the state would get on with only five praetors, and the election was cancelled. A generation later, in 148, Scipio Aemilianus had his name brought forward

[55] Nicolet (1976) 391. I find it rather odd that Nicolet flinches from the conclusion that seems to me to be imposed by the massive evidence he adduces.
[56] See briefly Harris (1979) 41–3.

for the consulship though ineligible on at least two counts. This time popular pressure forced the Senate and the presiding consul to concede despite their strong objections. How? The sources are both late and too brief to be directly informative, but Astin is surely right to infer that, in the absence of 'orderly and legal channels' by which the Senate could have been thwarted, 'some fairly substantial public outcry or disturbance' had taken place.[57] The same inference is in order to explain the passage nine years later of the first of a series of *leges tabellariae* introducing the secret ballot into, in turn, elections, judicial proceedings and legislative decisions.[58]

One other weapon in the armoury of the Roman ruling class requires some consideration, namely, its exclusive right to interpret supernatural signs and portents and to take the consequent practical steps. I stress the word 'right'. Divination was of course a widespread activity in the ancient world; our concern, however, is not with the intractable problems of belief but with the purely external matter of the impact of omens and portents on formal political behaviour. Stated simply, the Romans divided the year into *dies fasti*, when public business could legitimately be conducted, and *dies nefasti*, about one-third of the year, when it was taboo (except for meetings of the Senate).[59] The dates were on the whole fixed and therefore incorporated into the political timetable, but complications arose because days that were normally *fasti* could suddenly be declared to be in effect *nefasti* on account of a portent, such as an unfavourable flight of birds. A Voltairean catalogue can be compiled of occasions when that was done by Senate or magistrates in order to block an assembly meeting or the passage of a piece of legislation. No less revealing is a sort of reverse manipulation: in 193 B.C., for example, earthquakes (very bad portents) were so frequent that all public business came to a stop until the Senate forbade any further reporting of them (Livy 34.55). Such practices cannot be dismissed as mere cynicism, though a few contemporaries, exceptional men 'of quite extraordinary literary and philosophical culture', are on record to that effect. Behind the practice lay the notion, characteristic of the way Roman religion developed, that 'human interpretation of signs had as much if not more effect than the will of the gods sending the signs'.[60]

[57] Astin (1967) 66.   [58] See ch. 5 at nn. 30, 31.
[59] The fullest account will be found in Michels (1967), esp. ch. 3.
[60] Jocelyn (1966/7) 102–3; cf. Liebeschuetz (1979) 24–8.

It was equally characteristic of the Romans that this great power of interpretation, and indeed all aspects of official religion, were fully incorporated into the governmental apparatus; that the pontiffs, the augurs and the others entitled to perform sacrifices, organize cult activities and interpret the divine signs were men who also sat in the Senate and held magistracies, selected according to the same 'considerations of class solidarity and privilege'.[61] They were not rarely coopted for priestly office while still too young to qualify for the magistracies and some then went on to attain the consulship in time.[62] Neither in Athens nor in the other Greek city-states was there anything comparable. Although there too 'priests' were fully a part of the state apparatus, such prestige and perquisites as they may have had (little enough for those, the majority, who were chosen by lot for a one-year term like other officials) did not extend to political influence or even to the advancement of their own political careers.[63] Nor were they charged with the duty of public divination. Warde Fowler observed long ago that

our information about private divination is scattered about in Roman literature, and even when brought together there is not a great deal of it . . . In Greek literature exactly the opposite is the case; there we hear little of State-authorized divination, and a great deal of wandering soothsayers, soothsaying families, and oracles which (except at Delphi) were not under the direct control of a City-state.[64]

The difference in practice was a sharp one. Every public act in antiquity was preceded by an attempt to gain supernatural support, through prayers, sacrifices or vows, but the Romans also sought to divine the attitude of the gods in advance. The taking of auspices was a standard procedure; a declaration of unfavourable auspices was automatically accepted without dispute, so that in effect an augur possessed the power of 'veto on every public transaction'.[65] Greek states had no comparable officials and rarely consulted oracles or soothsayers; they left divination largely to private 'specialists' whose authority and predictions could always be challenged or disregarded. It is therefore not too surprising how rare are

[61] Jocelyn (1966/7) 92–4.
[62] D. E. Hahm, 'The Roman Nobility and the Three Major Priesthoods, 218–167 B.C.', *Transactions of the Amer. Philological Assn.* 94 (1963) 73–85.
[63] See D. D. Feaver, 'Historical Development in the Priesthoods of Athens', *Yale Classical Studies* 15 (1957) 123–58.
[64] Fowler (1911) 295–6.　　[65] Fowler (1911) 305.

the attested cases in Greek history of the temporary disruption of official business or of military activity in consequence of unfavourable portents.[66] The great double ill-omen of 415 B.C., the mutilation of the herms and 'profanation' of the Eleusinian mysteries, succeeded in bringing about the recall of Alcibiades from Sicily on a personal charge but it had no effect on the expedition itself. Four years later, when it was proposed to reinstate Alcibiades as general, the two families traditionally in charge of the mysteries, the Eumolpids and the Kerykes, objected 'in the name of the gods' (Thucydides 8.53.2). But they were not officials of the state, they had no right of veto and their protests went unheeded.

I have unavoidably simplified a complex situation, and also a paradoxical one. On the one hand, the religiosity of both Greeks and Romans was visible everywhere and on all occasions. Yet, although they of course recognized a category that the Romans called *ius sacrum*, there was in effect no canon law, for the *ius sacrum* was laid down and enforced by the same organs of the state as the civil law, though different experts may have been employed when technical advice was needed; the state had the right to punish offences against the gods, to censor or ban religious practices, organizations or beliefs, and, for all its usual tolerance, it did not hesitate to do so under pressure. On the other hand, government had become generally secularized in reality though not in appearance. The oath, for example, which had once been a formal proof in a dispute (e.g. Homer, *Iliad* 23.581-5), was reduced to a mere ceremony, though still required of all witnesses. It was now necessary to persuade the judges and jurymen; the threat that perjury would bring down the wrath of the gods was no longer of itself persuasive.[67] Many Greek communities selected their officials by lot as a matter of routine, without any suggestion that the choice was thereby being transferred to the gods.[68] If the Romans rejected

---

[66] On the military side, the rarity emerges clearly from the evidence collected by Pritchett (1971-9) III ch. 1-4; cf. H. Popp, *Die Einwirkung von Vorzeichen, Opfern und Festen auf die Kriegsführung der Griechen* . . . (Diss. Erlangen 1957). A recent claim that the history of the Sicilian expedition and therefore the fate of the Athenian empire 'were due . . . to the relations between the Athenians and the irrational' is simply silly: C. A. Powell, 'Religion and the Sicilian Expedition', *Historia* 28 (1979) 15-31.

[67] See K. Latte, *Heiliges Recht* (Tübingen 1920), pp. 37-9.

[68] See Headlam (1933) 4-12.

this procedure, that, too, was for reasons having nothing to do with religion.

In short, I can find no warrant for any notion of direct manipulation of religion in support of substantive programmes or interests of the ruling classes. Both the necessary doctrine and ecclesiastical organization were lacking. Nothing could be less true, less consonant with the evidence, than the view of Martin Nilsson about Greek political behaviour when he declared that oracles and omens 'were the most effective means to influence the man in the street who voted in the popular assembly'.[69] No doubt the vote of any given individual could have been decided by an oracle or soothsayer, but there is no important instance when the Delphic oracle determined a state's course of action (as distinct from providing a retrospective explanation of a failure); no known case of a genuine deflection of policy because of the protests of private diviners or oracle-mongers. In Rome, as we have seen, actions could be delayed by official interpretation of portents, but that is cold comfort for the Nilsson doctrine of a conflict between élite enlightenment and popular superstition. In Rome popular participation was sufficiently constrained without this additional weapon, the use of which is to be properly located in the context of personal rivalry between individuals or factions within the ruling élite.[70]

The vast body of religious practices was of course an integral part of the traditional *nomos* or *mos maiorum* that upheld the whole structure, including the right of the élite to dominate. The sacral aura of *fasces*, lictors and triumphs (noted in chapter 3) provides one illustration. But the further step was not taken to claim divine warrant for any specific magisterial or legislative decision. In the present context, the decisive fact is that though appeals to ancestral tradition were frequently heard in the constitutional crises, the gods were not invoked by those who were resisting or advocating change. Much as one hoped for divine support in an enterprise, no one argued that the gods were concerned with the substance of a political issue. When an augur cancelled an assembly meeting, he declared that the *day* was inauspicious for public business, not that

---

[69] M. P. Nilsson, *Cults, Myths, Oracles and Politics in Ancient Greece* (Lund 1951), p. 134. This approach is the central motif of Nilsson's *Greek Popular Religion* (New York 1940).
[70] Liebeschuetz (1979) 13–15; Jocelyn (1966/7) 96–7.

the *proposal* to be voted on had received divine disapproval. I find that a critical distinction. My 'Voltairean catalogue' was concentrated, at an accelerating rate, in the first century B.C., with an open cynicism and open factionalism, which, it has rightly been said, constituted one 'aspect of the collapse of the political institutions of the republic'.[71]

One reason, I believe, why historians of antiquity of recent generations have tended to evade a serious inquiry into politics is that much of ancient, and particularly Roman, politics looked like a pointless game to men steeped in a mythology of 'rational' politics, in which leaders and their supporters were what I have already called disembodied spirits, free from passions and prejudices. The experience of more recent decades has shown that there are few limits to the human capacity to accept weighted voting systems, interpretation of portents, charismatic leaders and all the rest as 'real' and legitimate operational devices, not as empty charades. What was (and is) essential is a belief, or at least a hope, that the devices and spectacles were part of a process leading to the achievement of social goals. Politics, in other words, were not just open-ended procedures; they were about issues, and that is the aspect we shall next consider systematically.

[71] Liebeschuetz (1979) 16.

5

POLITICAL ISSUES AND CONFLICT

Professional politicians, whether in the ancient Graeco-Roman or in the contemporary context, are quantitatively a negligible minority of the citizen-body. For them politics are a way of life, even though they believe, or at least persuade themselves, that their role is to advance the good of the society in which they operate; that, in other words, politics are a second-order activity designed to achieve objectives that are in themselves not political. For everyone else politics are wholly instrumental: the objectives themselves are what matter in the end. In saying that, I do not imply that there is no satisfaction, or anyway fun, in the excitement of an election campaign or a close legislative contest; or that Roman-style elections, with their massive games and handouts, did not offer immediate, tangible gains unconnected with policies or programmes. Nor do I suggest that 'the mass of citizens had clearly formulated goals in their minds or that they were less apt than their present-day counterparts to hold mutually contradictory views. I am saying no more than the commonplace that men who voted in elections or assemblies did not divorce personalities from issues, that they believed that in one way or another the issues mattered enough to them to warrant their participation in politics at some level.[1]

Yet, obvious though it seems, this assessment has been challenged by ancient historians from two opposing directions. Christian Meier, writing about Greece, and more particularly about Athens, says that there 'politics was so much a way of being (*Sein*), a way of life, that it could not have been a means to satisfy interests from other sectors of life'.[2] However, the common objection comes from the other direction, for example in Astin's conclusion that the 'energy and rivalry' expressed in Roman consular elections 'had very little to do with decisions of state, for the simple reason that

---

[1] See Finley (1976*a*).

[2] Meier (1980) 258. He here rejects my view of politics as instrumental without any explicit examination of my grounds for taking such a position.

election or rejection of particular candidates could rarely determine such decisions', that the Roman people 'in their votes rarely influenced policy'.[3] Although he confined this judgment to consular elections in the period 200–167 B.C. and presumably would not extend it automatically to all other periods, certainly not to decisions in the assemblies on substantive measures, I have doubts about any approach that erects a barrier between candidates as personalities and candidates as embodiments of policies. Certainly it is true that the Senate, the government, did not shift policies with every annual consular election, and that often enough the choice between any two candidates had no meaningful policy implications. But that is not the point at issue. The question is rather if the mass of voters thought that it mattered, somehow, whether X was elected or Y, regardless of the realism or folly of their thinking. It does not help to inject the truism that 'the voters' is an abstraction, that different voters had different reasons for the choices they made. If their decisions were influenced, consciously or subconsciously, rightly or wrongly, by the attribution of a programme, a posture, a course of action to a political figure, then the effectiveness or otherwise of their votes and the differences in judgment among them do not serve to deny that they had 'decisions of state' in view. If, furthermore, they felt an interest in the choice of decisions, then I am right to say that for them politics were instrumental.

The decades with which Astin was concerned, 200–167 B.C. (covered by the last fifteen surviving books of Livy's *History*), were dominated in foreign affairs by the wars and diplomatic manoeuvres in the east, in Macedonia, Greece and Asia Minor. Livy's narrative is filled with uncertainties in Rome about the aims and potentialities of these new and largely unknown opponents, with a considerable oscillation in tactics towards the eastern enemies and allies alike, with a slowness of decision about long-term policies (in so far as they were envisaged at all). We shall never know, except for one or two occasions and in the most superficial way, how much debate there was over specific policies, how much the leading contenders for office identified themselves with one or another tactic or policy, or what public opinion was in these matters. What I cannot believe is that the electoral contests and military operations were a game for

---

[3] Astin (1968) 10–11; cf. Veyne (1976) 419–26.

honour and booty, for titles and triumphs, and nothing else.[4] The
declaration of war against Macedon met popular opposition in 200
B.C., and there was localized trouble with the call-up in 193, 191
and 171. There were important domestic measures and conflicts:
criminal trials in 196 (not for the first time) on charges of violating
the laws limiting pasturage on 'public land'; repeal of a sumptuary
law in 195; a law in 193 designed to prevent evasion of the Roman
usury laws by the introduction of non-Roman 'partners' into loan
transactions; the expulsion in 187 and again in 177 of large numbers
of Latins who had legally migrated to the city of Rome and thereby
acquired Roman citizenship; the Bacchanalian affair of 186; more
sumptuary measures and scandals over the letting of public contracts during Cato's censorship (of 184 B.C.) and again in 169; the
lex annalis of 180, which tried to regularize the *cursus honorum*;
wholesale removal of illegal squatters from the Campanian *ager
publicus* in 172.

I have restricted myself to an incomplete listing within the period
200–167. So far as we know, in those years of extensive settlement
of Romans in colonies within Italy there was no general crisis over
landholdings, as there had been earlier and as there was to be on a
grand scale a few decades later; and resistance to the call-up had not
yet reached the intensity of 151 and 138, when the tribunes
imprisoned the consuls in order to block the levy. They were years
that fell within what Brunt has called the 'era of quiescence,
287–134', during which, he explains, 'popular agitation' had 'almost
ceased'.[5] But quiescence and agitation are relative concepts, and we
are in danger of falling into the trap set by the unavoidable habit of
historians concerned with distant ages to foreshorten time, to think
in half-centuries, centuries, even millennia. The historian's subjects,
however, lived in years and decades, not centuries, and they did not
live in a permanent state of street riots and civil war. That would
have meant the end of politics and a political society. Quiescence in
the sense of absence of civil war therefore does not of itself imply
absence of political conflict, any more than agitation disappears
because there are no, or few, large-scale riots. Political conflict
takes different forms, and that too requires explanation: one must

---

[4] The classic statement of the view I am contesting is that of Syme (1939) 11: 'The
political life of the Roman Republic was stamped and swayed, not by parties and
programmes . . . but by the strife for power, wealth and glory.'
[5] Brunt (1971a) 13.

consider why there were long periods of such quiescence and other periods of turbulence.

For the years 200–167 (chosen only because they were Astin's subject), my list includes a sufficient number of occasions when interests were seriously touched, when disagreement and conflict can reasonably be assumed, even though they fell short of armed riots and 'secessions'. Direct evidence is largely lacking, thanks to the nature of our main source, Livy's *History*. He dismisses the popular opposition to the declaration of war in 200 B.C. with the contemptuous remark (31.6.3) that the tribune Q. Baebius resorted to the old tactic (*via antiqua*) of abusing the *patres* for entering into one war after another and denying the plebs the enjoyment of peace. Was there no public agitation? His long account of the Bacchanalian affair (39.8–19) is a lurid tale of conspiracy and unnatural rites, with little factual detail, concentrating on the heroic efforts of Senate and consuls to save Rome and ignoring the views and behaviour of the ordinary citizens. The two expulsions of Latins from the city are attributed solely to the complaints of the Latin communities about their own loss of manpower (39.3.4–6; 41.8–9). Was there no problem in Rome itself, economic or political, because of this large influx? Other measures I have mentioned are reported blandly, in a sentence or two merely recording the action taken. Only once is there a significant exception: the repeal in 195 of a sumptuary law restricting women's carriages and ornaments was helped, if not imposed, by large-scale public demonstrations (34.1–8), and I take it that this information is given solely because of the considerable participation of women in the demonstrations, a notable departure from traditional decorous behaviour.

That mass opinion made little direct impact on the Roman ruling class at this time is no doubt true, but it does not follow from the impotence of the people (or from Livy's silences) that the citizenry at large had no interest in matters of policy and made no attempt to indicate their views, or that the contestants for high position did not allow those views to enter into their own calculations (and behaviour). Roman candidates and voters alike would have been unique in the history of political societies if they had completely separated self-interest from public interest. Sincerity, logical consistency, effectiveness are all beside the point in this context. Analysis can only be hindered by concern with the motives or sincerity of Flaminius or the Gracchi, not to mention Alcibiades in Athens and Julius Caesar at the end of the Republic.

The actor's perception of interests, his own, those of his class or section of the population, those of his country, is of course a complicated one, often self-contradictory to the eye of the observer when not to the actor himself. In a world in which war was a normal part of life, with its powerful overtone of national interest and patriotism, the common contradiction between ideological expressions of value and responses to individual practical measures (so well documented in our own society[6]) would have found frequent outlet, as in the request by citizens of the maritime colonies for exemption from naval service in 191 B.C. (Livy 36.3.5). Other obvious contradictions were between short-term and long-term interests, and between individual and class (or sectional) interests – too obvious to require extended comment. Nevertheless, slippery and confused as self-assessment of interest and the consequent behaviour may have been, it is possible to chart with some precision the main areas of political conflict among sectors of the population and the underlying drives. It is also possible to examine Greece and Rome together once again, for the issues were sufficiently similar, much as the final outcome of the conflicts diverged.

The obvious starting-point is constitutional conflict, and in no area does the existence of two different levels of intensity seem more evident. One was the level of outright struggle for power: the lower classes fought, often literally, for a share in government, and where they succeeded the upper classes sought to regain the political monopoly they had lost. The cycle of constitutions (*metabole politeion*) became an obsession among Greek political analysts from the mid-fifth century B.C.[7] It occurs throughout Aristotle's *Politics* and the 158 booklets on individual 'constitutions' compiled by him and his school (all now lost except the one on Athens). As late as the second century B.C. the Greek Polybius was baffled by the Roman success in escaping it.[8] Underneath lay the fact obvious to everyone that constitutions were very unstable even in their own day. In city after city there was an oscillation between oligarchy and democracy, accompanied by civil war, wholesale killing, exile and confiscation. Sometimes tyrants intervened, adding another dimension to

---

[6] See briefly Finley (1973*b*) 62–3, with references.
[7] The standard account is Ryffel (1949).
[8] See most recently Nippel (1980) 142–53.

the cycle. The other level of conflict, the 'quiescent' one, was marked by changes within the existing constitutional framework, a process that never ceased and that sometimes involved more agitation and resistance than such a colourless word as 'adjustment' might suggest. Much as the two levels differed at their extremes, there was a large blurred area of overlap.

In concluding the historical section of his *Constitution of Athens* (ch. 41), Aristotle counted eleven transformations, beginning with two legendary ones under Ion and Theseus and the dubious reforms of Draco, followed by the Solonic reforms, the tyranny of the Pisistratids, the Cleisthenic constitution, the take-over of leadership by the Council of the Areopagus during the Persian wars, the removal of the Areopagus from power by Ephialtes, the oligarchic coup in 411 B.C., the overthrow of the oligarchy a year later, the tyranny of the Thirty at the end of the Peloponnesian War, and the final restoration of democracy in 403 B.C. There are difficulties with this picture but, details apart, there is no disputing either the reappearance of the level of unquiet struggle at the end of the fifth century, halfway through the classical period, or the sometimes blurred division between quiet and violent conflict. Athens may have been on the brink of civil war when Solon was given plenipotentiary powers but there is no hint in the tradition of actual fighting; the way in which Ephialtes was able to achieve critical changes has gone unreported and so there is an impression of 'peacefulness', but the fact that he was assassinated leaves doubts; the oligarchic coup of 411 B.C. as described by Thucydides was accomplished by a classic mixture of propaganda and terror.

Then there were many measures that did not bring about a transformation, a *metabole*, but were of great importance in the shaping of the Athenian system in the course of the fifth century: changes in the method of selecting *strategoi* and archons, which elevated the former and degraded the latter (and the polemarch), extension of eligibility for the archonship to the third Solonic census-class, the *zeugitai*, the marriage law of 451/0 restricting citizenship to the children of two citizen-parents, pay for office, the creation of a board of accountants (*logistai*) to check outgoing officials, the introduction of the *graphe paranomon*, the disappearance of ostracism, and at the end of the century the recodification of the laws and the introduction of *nomothesia*. It is inconceivable that these, and other measures, were adopted without opposition, debate, agitation and conflict; yet for many of them our ignorance extends even to the date of introduction.

I have excluded from my list debates and conflicts over foreign and military policy, war and empire. For the other Greek city-states such an exclusion would effectively reduce one to silence about politics, with the exception of Syracuse in brief periods, a most untypical instance thanks to the survival of chunks of Timaeus' *History* in the work of Diodorus.[9] Even when we are told about constitutional transformations, as is not rarely the case, there are no meaningful details and often no certainty about the dates when they occurred. That is true of classical Sparta before the reigns of Agis and Cleomenes in the third century B.C.; of Argos despite enough scattered data to provide us with a fleshless skeleton of its constitutional structure;[10] of fifth-century Chios and Samos because of (rather than despite) the elliptical statements by Thucydides,[11] and of Thebes despite the lengthy accounts in Xenophon's *Hellenica* and in Plutarch of the manoeuvrings round Epaminondas and Pelopidas in the fourth century B.C.[12] Of the hundreds of other *poleis*, larger (Corinth, Acragas) or smaller, there is effectively no information. The situation is adequately summed up in the opening sentences of Amit's three case-studies of long-term conflicts between large and small *poleis*: 'We possess almost no independent knowledge (other than archaeological) of the history of Aegina. The island appears in historical texts mainly in connection with its relations with Athens.'[13]

Nothing short of a miraculous recovery of Aristotle's 157 lost *Constitutions* will radically alter the position. In his surviving works, he offers no more than fragmented, undated and often unclear, scattered examples of incidents that triggered civil strife and of devices employed. Two passages in the *Politics* about

---

[9] See Finley (1979) ch. 5–8.
[10] M. Wörrle, *Untersuchungen zur Verfassungsgeschichte von Argos im 5. Jahrhundert vor Christus* (Diss. Erlangen–Nuremberg 1964). The brief relevant chapters (18–19) in R. A. Tomlinson, *Argos and the Argolid* (London 1972), are short on facts, long on fantasy.
[11] Hence the continuing, unsuccessful attempts by modern scholars to find order in the chaos, most recently by J. L. O'Neil, 'The Constitution of Chios in the Fifth Century B.C.', *Talanta* 10/11 (1978–79) 66–73; W. Schuller, 'Die Einführung der Demokratie auf Samos im 5. Jahrhundert v. Chr.', *Klio* 63 (1981) 281–8.
[12] See the narrative by P. Cloché, *Thèbes de Béotie* (Publ. de la Fac. de Philosophie et Lettres de Namur 13, n.d.).
[13] M. Amit, *Great and Small Poleis* (Brussels 1973), p. 9.

Massalia (Marseilles) are paradigmatic. The first (1305b2–12) reads as follows:

Sometimes an oligarchy is destroyed by rich men who are excluded from office, when the office-holders are few in number, as happened in Istros, Heraclea, Massalia and other *poleis*. Those excluded from office agitated until a share was given first to the elder brothers [in a family], later to the younger . . . And so in Massalia the oligarchy became more communal (*politikoteros*), in Istros it finally ended in democracy, in Heraclea it broadened from a few to six hundred.

Later on in the volume Aristotle explains (1321a26–35) that

there are various ways in which an oligarchy can give the masses (*to plethos*) a share in the civic organization (*politeuma*) . . . for instance, as in Massalia, by making a selection of those who are worthy both within and outside the *politeuma*.

Everyone is free to guess what Aristotle had in mind (impeded by the unresolved vagueness of his notion of a form of government he called *politeia* that was neither oligarchy nor democracy but more desirable than either), when these actions were supposed to have occurred or what kind of constitution Massalia had in Aristotle's own day. The next reference is considerably more than a century later, when an inscription of 195 B.C. from Lampsacus in Asia Minor mentions a body of Massaliot officials called *timouchoi*;[14] then we must wait another century and a half for some empty phrases in Cicero, Caesar (and other Latin writers of the next two generations) praising the existing aristocratic regime of Massalia, and for a sentence in the Greek geographer Strabo (4.1.5) explaining that there were 600 *timouchoi* with life tenure who constituted a council, headed by an executive committee of fifteen and a still smaller executive of three. The modern historians' game of making bricks without straw is not hindered: the most recent player concludes that for five and a half centuries 'an aristocracy of birth and wealth always had the power' in Massalia 'without a single disturbance, a single demand from the side of the people ever being mentioned'.[15] That reveals total deafness to Aristotle's language,

---

[14] *Sylloge inscriptionum graecarum*, 3 ed., 591.45, 49.

[15] M. Clavel, 'Das griechische Marseille. Entwicklungsstufen und Dynamik einer Handelsmacht', in *Hellenische Poleis*, ed. E. C. Welskopf (4 vols., Berlin 1974) II 855–969, at pp. 902–7. The most reasonable attempt at a reconstruction was made by E. Lepore, 'Struttura della colonizzazione focea in Occidente', *Parola del Passato* 25 (1970) 20–54, at pp. 44–53, but my scepticism remains.

but my interest is rather in the methodological fallacy – to which we shall have to return – of assuming that our source-record is so complete, generation by generation, that such an argument from silence is worth something.

When we turn from the Greek world to Italy north of the Bay of Naples, any inquiry into politics is blocked by almost total silence, whether about the Etruscans or the Samnites or the other Italic peoples, before and after they entered the Roman power sphere. Rome alone constitutes an exception. The more than two centuries from the creation of the Republic to the lex Hortensia of 287 B.C., which gave statutory status to *plebiscita*, measures adopted by the plebeian assembly (*concilium plebis*), are regularly headed 'the struggle between the orders' in books on Roman history. But what does 'struggle' mean? What forms did it take? The early books of Livy are filled with tales of public demonstrations, riots and street fighting, and three times, in 494, 449 and 287, the plebs 'seceded', that is to say, they refused military service until a particular measure was adopted. On the other hand, Livy not infrequently identifies periods of *concordia ordinum* (e.g. 7.27.1) or he reports the passage of important measures, such as the law of 357 setting one twelfth as the maximum rate of interest (7.16.1), in the most casual way, without any hint of accompanying disorder. I bow to no man in my disbelief in Livy's narrative, not to mention the stories of Dionysius of Halicarnassus or Plutarch, but I believe the overall pattern to be correct. That is to say, two centuries of continuous riotous struggle are an impossibility in an organized, functioning society, whether in Rome or anywhere else. There were years of peak intensity when civil war might have broken out, but most years were 'quiescent', years during which the process of constitutional change proceeded, at uneven tempo, by political manoeuvring within the ruling class against a background of popular discontent.

All levels of intensity were embraced by the splendid Greek portmanteau-word *stasis*. When employed in a social–political context, *stasis* had a broad range of meanings, from political grouping or rivalry through faction (in its pejorative sense) to open civil war. That correctly reflected the political realities. Ancient moralists and theorists, who were hostile to the realities, understandably clung to the pejorative overtones of the word and identified *stasis* as the central malady of their society. It is, however, not comprehensible why modern historians follow their lead, as does the Liddell-and-Scott Lexicon when it defines *stasis* as a 'party formed for seditious purposes'. That is simply false: 'seditious' is not a necessary overtone, though a possible one in specific cases.[16] To be sure, the aim of any *stasis* was to bring about a change in some law or arrangement, and any change meant a loss of rights, privileges or wealth to some group, faction or class, for whom the *stasis* was accordingly seditious. But from that standpoint all politics are seditious in any society in which there is a measure of popular participation, of freedom for political manoeuvring.[17]

It is wrong, in sum, to divide the history of the ancient city-states into long neatly demarcated periods of either 'struggle' or 'quiescence'. However, a certain pattern can be discovered. The long years of transformation from the archaic aristocratic monopoly to the classical city-state structure necessarily required moments of sharp struggle, even civil war, separated by longer and quieter periods of agitation. Then a fundamental divergence developed: in states in which the new system was sufficiently stabilized, continuing political conflict was on the whole contained well short of extreme *stasis*; but in many states, perhaps most, that level of stability was never reached, and so there was the frequent, bloody oscillation between oligarchy and democracy, or between one oligarchic faction and another. The main variable was the extent of stabilization; that is what requires explanation, and I find it in the fact that the successful conquest-states, Sparta, Athens, Rome, were also the stable ones (in the specific sense in which I am here employing that concept). War as such was not a variable because it was an omnipresent activity. What mattered was the outcome of continuing warfare, above all, the consequences for the peasant majority. In the end, Brunt has correctly noted, 'the course of the revolution in which the Republic fell was decided by the soldiers, who were nearly all recruited from the country folk'.[18] In the preceding centuries the same country folk had made possible both the Roman conquests and the relative stability of the state.

I thus return to a point with which I began this chapter, the instrumentality of politics. 'No man', said a client of Lysias (25.8) at the beginning of the fourth century B.C., 'is an oligarch or a

---

[16] That has been demonstrated by Loenen (1953), a neglected analysis that is not even listed in the 8½-page bibliography in Lintott (1982).

[17] See briefly Finley (1976a) 6–8.   [18] Brunt (1971a) 8.

democrat by nature; it is out of interest that he supports a regime.'
This was a world dominated by low technology, small peasant
holdings, small workshops and street traders, hence always on the
edge of disaster in the countryside and of food shortages in the
cities. What did it matter to the mass of the citizenry in Athens
whether archons were elected or chosen by lot, in Rome whether
the consulship was or was not open to men of plebeian origins, in
either city whether or not they had effective voting strength in the
assemblies, except in so far as the constitutional arrangements
enhanced the possibility of decisions that would be in their interest?

Roughly their interests fell into two broad areas. One was their
power (in a formal sense) to defend themselves and their rights at
law. This was a subject of particularly sharp conflict in the archaic
period, while the law was not written down and judicial authority
was monopolized by a small closed aristocratic order. The struggle
over the XII Tables in Rome is the most spectacular and bitter one
known to us, but the shadowy tradition of the Greek 'lawgivers'
reflects the same situation. Aristotle (*Constitution of Athens* 9.1)
concluded that of all Solon's measures, three were most in the
interest of the common people: the abolition of debt bondage, the
right given to a third party to intervene in a lawsuit on behalf of
someone who had been wronged, and the introduction of appeal to
the courts. It is the second that interests me here. No classical state
ever established a sufficient governmental machinery by which to
secure the appearance of a defendant in court or the execution of a
judgment in private suits. Reliance on self-help was therefore
compulsory and it is obvious that such a situation created unfair
advantages whenever the opponents were unequal in the resources
they could command.[19] The Solonic measure and such Roman
institutions as the *vindex* (or against magistrates, the tribunes) were
designed to reduce the grosser disparities, characteristically by the
employment of a patronage device rather than by state machinery.
Publication of the laws was a step in the same direction, and the
resistance to it suggests that its value to the lower classes, and
indeed to all citizens who were outside the closed ruling circle, was
more than purely formal.

[19] See Egon Weiss, *Griechisches Privatrecht* (Leipzig 1923) bk IV; Kelly (1966), esp.
ch. 1; and the classic analysis by R. von Jhering, 'Reich und Arm im altrömischen
Civilprozess', in his *Scherz und Ernst in der Jurisprudenz* (3 ed., Leipzig 1885),
pp. 175ff.

But the substance, the 'mould' of the law, as we have seen, remained heavily biased. Not even democratized Greek courts removed the harshness of the law of debt, and still less the Romans, whose judiciary in private disputes continued to be monopolized by members of the élite. And the law of debt was perhaps the most critical single point in the area we are examining. The same can of course be said about the law through the whole of history: substantive inequality before the law has been accepted by the weaker classes as a fact of life, while they struggled, when they did, on other fronts, for tangible material gains rather than formal privileges. In agrarian societies that meant, above all, relief from the burden of debt – the fact of indebtedness, not just the legal formalities – and from land hunger. These two issues together – they were often joined in moments of crisis – constituted the second broad area of interests that political gains were expected to advance. Although the Greek evidence has finally been assembled and fully analysed (for the first time in the 1960s),[20] discussion is still befogged by modern ideological stances. If on the one side there is perhaps less nonsense being written than heretofore about the evils of ancient 'socialism',[21] there remains on the other side a paradoxically stultifying suspicion of our sources and their upper-class orientation.

It is only too easy to brush aside generalized or rhetorical comments – in Plato (*Laws* 3.684D-E, 5.736C-E), for example, in Isocrates (12.259), or in Polybius (6.9.9) – about the revolutionary slogan, 'Cancel debts and redistribute the land.' It is no less easy to ridicule, say, Diodorus' summary account (15.58) of the *stasis* in Argos in 370 B.C.: an oligarchic coup was secretly planned because demagogues were stirring up the masses against the wealthy; the plotters were betrayed; 1,200 were executed without proper trial and their property confiscated; finally the bloodthirsty mob put the demagogues to death, too. 'So', Diodorus concludes, 'they received the punishment fitting their crimes . . . and the *demos*, relieved of their madness, were restored to their good senses.'

Distrust of such sources is certainly justified – but distrust, not

---

[20] D. Asheri, *Distribuzioni di terre nell' antica Grecia* (Memorie dell' Accademia delle Scienze di Torino, Classe di scienze morali . . ., ser. 4, no. 10, 1966), and 'Leggi greche sul problema dei debiti', *Studi classici e orientali* 18 (1969) 5–122.

[21] E.g. Pöhlmann (1925) I 322–419, II 437–63; A. Passerini, 'Riforme sociali e divisione di beni nella Grecia del IV secolo', *Athenaeum*, n.s. 8 (1930) 273–98.

neglect. Not all narrative references are as tendentious as the one from Diodorus about Argos: there is no way, for example, to get round Thucydides' brief references to the distribution of property confiscated in Leontini (5.4) and Samos (8.21) during the Peloponnesian War, in both cases directly linked with political revolutions. Nor can suspicion about the possible ideological distortions of a Plato or an Isocrates be extended to official documents: the oath taken by Athenian jurors included 'I will not allow the cancellation of private debts or the redistribution of land or houses belonging to Athenian citizens'; so did the oath required of all the citizens of Cretan Itanos early in the third century B.C.; an early fourth-century Delphic law on moneylending carried the final sanction that anyone seeking to abrogate the law should be subject to the same curse as anyone proposing redistribution of land or cancellation of debts; the league of Greek states founded at Corinth in 338 B.C. under the leadership of Philip of Macedon decreed that in no city-state 'shall there be . . . confiscation of property or redistribution of land or cancellation of debts or freeing of slaves for purposes of revolution'.[22] Such programmatic statements, supported by oaths and maledictions, are unlikely to have been adopted on the basis of purely imaginary fears.

Now it is a fact that we have very few such explicit statements, even fewer instances on record of a total concellation of debts (as in Solon's so-called *seisachtheia*) or of a total redistribution of a community's land. However, 'redistribution of land and cancellation of debts' is a Utopian slogan. Land can be made available to the landless outside the territory of the city-state (what we call colonization) or there can be partial redistribution, that is, of property confiscated from the victims of a *stasis* (as in Leontini and Samos, already mentioned). The burden of debt can be reduced by the abolition of debt-bondage, by restriction of interest rates or by moratoria. Once we direct our attention away from Utopian schemes, the argument from silence collapses, even with our highly random selection of available texts. Ancient writers were not wrong, in sum, to assume that grievances over land and debt were standing in the wings whenever there was a political conflict in which the poor were involved more or less directly; or to reflect

---

[22] The respective references are Demosthenes 24.149; *Inscriptiones Creticae* III iv, 8.21–4; *Fouilles de Delphes* III 1, 294; Pseudo-Demosthenes 17.15.

upper-class fears that radical demands might emerge from the wings onto the stage. Substantive issues, I submit, lay behind popular interest in constitutional reforms and elections, in political conflicts. Ordinary Greeks and Romans, like ordinary people everywhere, were not egalitarian Utopians. Even when roused to the extremes of civil war and strikes against military conscription, in the end they usually accepted 'reformist' measures, patronage devices to secure protection in legal disputes rather than more far-ranging changes in the law itself, abolition of debt-bondage, moratoria and interest maxima rather than cancellation of debts, colonization when that was possible rather than redistribution of land. This last alternative was perhaps the best safety-valve against civil war and the key to political 'quiescence' and stability.

Archaic Greece from the earliest times, as far back as the mid-eighth century B.C., saw a continuous dispersal of Greeks to new settlements in foreign lands (for which 'colonies' is a misnomer), extending to Marseilles and down the Spanish coast in the west and to the Crimea and the eastern end of the Black Sea in the north east. It is impossible from the miserable ancient accounts that survive to examine the politics of this movement, and it is anyway doubtful that one may properly speak of politics at this embryonic stage of the city-state. One can reasonably surmise no more than that so many venturesome emigrations in small groups reflected conflict at home, renewed in some cities time and again (most notably in Miletus) and sometimes, perhaps often, involving forcible expulsion.[23] One may also surmise that a *demos* that was becoming more and more politically conscious, say by the sixth century, was also increasingly unwilling to accept such a solution to their land hunger. Nor was suitable territory available without limits, as the good coastal lands on the Mediterranean and Black Sea shores were occupied, and as Etruscans and Carthaginians blocked further settlement and some native peoples also found themselves able to resist (notably the Italic peoples of southern Italy).

[23] The only certainly attested case of forcible emigration is the colonization of Cyrene from Thera: Herodotus 4.153 and *Supplementum Epigraphicum Graecum* IX 3, taken together. Ancient claims for Milesian colonies reached as high as ninety: Pliny, *Natural History* 5.112; see F. Bilabel, *Die ionische Kolonisation* (*Philologus*, Supp. XIV 1, 1920), ch. 1. Although such a figure need not be believed, any realistic reduction would still justify my statement about repeated conflict.

Very few Greek communities had the power to seek an external solution nearer home by conquest: Sparta most notably, with peculiar consequences; tyrants in Sicily and southern Italy, who massacred or transplanted populations almost at will; and Athens with its plantation of 'cleruchies' on confiscated foreign territory. No one, I think, will dispute that the final subjugation of Messenia late in the seventh century B.C., its extensive agricultural land divided among the Spartiates, was an essential factor in Sparta's freedom from *stasis* for nearly three hundred years. In Athens during the imperial period perhaps ten thousand citizens – 8 or 10 per cent of the whole citizen body – were settled in cleruchies or were assigned arbitrary and substantial 'rents' from estates retained and worked by the conquered population. So valuable was this outlet that the weaker Athens of the fourth century tried to repeat the performance, with some success for a time. About the hundreds of other Greek city-states, who lacked this power, we can say almost nothing in any meaningful detail. We cannot say, for example, how important a steady leakage of landless men may have been, by continued, if scattered, emigration to the more distant Greek settlements or by joining mercenary bands. Nor, as we have seen, can we give a statistical picture of *stasis*. But we can say that *stasis* was a permanent threat, appearing in the record, when it does, as a political or constitutional conflict; not only between oligarchy and democracy but also between factions within either camp. Not infrequently the outcome was tyranny, and to that extent the tyrants were also part of the history of classical politics.[24]

The Roman story on this score needs only the briefest outline-statement. From the beginning of the Republic to the end and then on into the Empire, both the burden of debt and the distribution of land were constant issues. In the early centuries, the struggle over debt was one about debt-bondage, and though its overt form (through the practice known as *nexum*) was eliminated by legislation in 326 B.C., more subtle types remained in existence throughout later Roman history.[25] There was also persistent con-

---

[24] The attempt by Lintott (1982) to provide a narrative of *stasis* between 750 and 330 B.C. is vitiated by his restriction of *stasis* to open violence (e.g., the conflict that brought Solon into action was only 'incipient civil strife', p. 43), by his uncritical use of the sources, and by the obvious inadequacy of the evidence for such an enterprise.

[25] On debt bondage see Finley (1981) ch. 9; on the persistence of what may be called quasi-debt-bondage, Finley (1976b) 112–17.

cern about interest rates and there were occasional debt 'crises' requiring serious governmental interference.[26] The struggle over landholding was no less, perhaps even more, persistent: on the one hand, the settlement of Romans and 'Latins' in colonies, invariably on territory taken from subjugated people, which began in the earliest Republic and never came to a halt; on the other hand, individual holdings on conquered land, which stimulated conflicts between the orders because of the upper-class tendency to occupy as much of this *ager publicus* as they could.[27] Some idea of the scale of this activity is offered by the following estimate: by the beginning of the second Punic War in 218 B.C., at least 9,000 km² of land had been assigned to colonists or individual settlers (approximately ten times the total territory of Rome at the end of the fifth century), and another 10,000 km² had been otherwise sold off or rented out.[28]

My interest, of course, is not in the economic history of Rome (or Greece) as such but in the issues that stimulated or exacerbated political conflict. Brunt has estimated that 50,000 small farms were created for Romans and Latins in the generation after 200 B.C. (the same generation that we looked at in some detail earlier),[29] whereas the following generation, which came to a close with the agrarian law and then the assassination of Tiberius Gracchus, saw a virtual cessation of colonization. That second generation was one of growing popular agitation, little as the available sources tell us about it. The series of so-called *leges tabellariae* from 139 B.C. on, introducing the secret ballot so disliked by the élite, clearly 'indicated rising discontent with the government of the nobility'.[30] One noble who supported the radical innovation was Scipio Aemilianus, whose election to the consulship by popular pressure against the wishes of the Senate we have already noticed. Even earlier, there was repeated resistance to conscription. Previous

---

[26] For one such crisis, see M. W. Frederiksen, 'Caesar, Cicero and the Problem of Debt', *Journal of Roman Studies* 56 (1966) 128–41.

[27] On the long pre-Gracchan history of conflict over the *ager publicus*, see G. Tibiletti, 'Il possesso dell' *ager publicus* e le norme *de modo agrorum* sino ai Gracchi', *Athenaeum*, n.s. 26 (1948) 173–235, 27 (1949) 2–41.

[28] Harris (1979) 60. The literary evidence for Roman colonization is set out concisely in *An Economic Survey of Ancient Rome*, ed. T. Frank, 1 (Baltimore 1933).

[29] Brunt (1971a) 64.

[30] Brunt (1971a) 66. On the secret ballot, see above all Nicolet (1970).

troubles over the levy, apart from the 'secessions', the first two of which the tradition specifically attributes to the debt-bondage issue, 'seem to have resulted mainly from well-founded grievances felt by particular groups'.[31] Now, from the 160s on, generalized lower-class opposition became widespread, at least to specific wars. That the agrarian and military manpower problems were indissolubly linked from the time of the Gracchi is too familiar to require further comment. What I am suggesting is that the nature and shape of Roman politics were always closely bound up with war, conquest and land settlement, that shifts between periods of 'agitation' and 'quiescent' times were both causes and consequences of specific political behaviour.

No one in the city-state world, and certainly no social class, was opposed to war, conquest and empire.[32] The extraordinary willingness of citizen militias to be conscripted and to fight year after year is sufficient witness. There were of course disagreements over tactical questions, whether or not to embark on a particular war or campaign, or when and on what terms to sign a peace agreement. Not even Sparta was immune, as over the question of going to war with Athens in 431 B.C. Such tactical debates were, by their nature, a matter for the political and military leaders of the community to conduct, even when the decision rested with a popular assembly. Thucydides (6.24.3–4) may have been very angry about the failure of Nicias to head off the Sicilian expedition, but he himself recorded that the final vote was unanimous, or at least *nem. con.* No clashing interests are detectable. And we have already noticed that the Senate or the magistrates commanding in the field regularly made such decisions in Rome; it is a methodological fallacy to convert into a pattern of class disagreement the handful of instances when the people rejected a senatorial decision.

To untangle the motivations of this unceasing hunger for war and conquest is not easy. Proper allowance must be made for such psychological or strategic considerations as patriotism, military glory, national interest, national defence; also to the hopes for personal booty. For most of the small Greek city-states and Italic 'tribes' there was nothing else to be gained. For Athens and Rome, however, there was another prospect, decisive in understanding

---

[31] Harris (1979) 48.
[32] See R. Meiggs, *The Athenian Empire* (Oxford 1972), ch. 21; Harris (1979) ch. 1.

their politics, namely, the material benefits of empire. In Athens they were varied, with conquered land a significant component; in Rome, land and settlement became the dominant factor. I do not imply that individual citizens attending the assembly made their decisions on a simple calculation of their chances of subsequently acquiring so many acres of land confiscated from the enemy. But I do suggest that Athenian cleruchies and what the Romans called 'public land' were never far beneath the surface of consciousness among the citizenry when some question involving conquest or empire was being discussed; that in foreign affairs this kind of interest was pivotal in the popular response to what often appears on the surface to be no more than personal quarrels within the élite for glory and power.

Isocrates knew what he was doing when in proposing a pan-Hellenic invasion of the Persian empire under the leadership of Philip of Macedon he stressed the opportunity for opening up vast new territories for settlement. The Roman ruling class knew what it was doing with its continuing programme of colonization. When it allowed narrow self-interest to shape its judgment over the *ager publicus*, political conflict repeatedly became *stasis* in its more extreme sense. It was a continuation of the same pattern when, during the final century of the Republic, the contenders for power were compelled to find land for their veterans at almost any price as a condition of retaining their personal military strength in the civil-war situation that had replaced traditional politics. The 'price' finally included considerable settlement in colonies outside Italy, a practice that had previously been so unpopular that it was barely attempted before Julius Caesar.[33]

There were times when an external agent distorted the situation and reduced all considerations to one of survival – the threat of Philip of Macedon, for example, or the invasion of Italy by Hannibal. Otherwise, however, the foreign policy of the stable conquest-states was a remarkably coherent and consistent one over a long duration, coloured from time to time by domestic political troubles but not diverted by them into substantially new directions. There is a common misconception on this subject, derived from the unsupported premise that 'an assembly of some three hundred persons [the Roman Senate] is not the ideal instrument for planning

---

[33] See Brunt (1971*b*) ch. 12.

complicated policies, let alone for applying them effectively and consistently over a substantial period';[34] and presumably demonstrated by such periods of indecision as the years in Athens of the rise of Philip of Macedon or of the first major Roman wars with Greece and the eastern monarchs in the early decades of the second century B.C. The fallacy is to assume perfect knowledge on the part of policy-makers (whoever they were), absolute predictability of the consequences of their actions, and the vision of a clear and precise long-term objective. On those assumptions, no state in history, whether ruled by a despot or by an assembly of three hundred, has had a consistent policy over a substantial period. I find it revealing that it was precisely in the decades of uncertainty about eastern policy that Rome created some 50,000 small farms for settlers. That was genuine continuity.

The rhetoric about 'the good old days' also makes its contribution to misunderstanding: historians seem little less immune than politicians and moralists. During the centuries of stability there were constant changes in the constitutional machinery without revolution, as we have seen. There were also changes in political activity and behaviour, shifting class relations, a greater or lesser ability of some interests to make themselves felt in the decision-making, perhaps changes in the intensity of political participation, and so on. That is all commonplace: it has been true of every political society. But why is change always for the worse, a sign of decline, of 'crisis'? For Athens it is impossible even to locate the 'good old days', given that a mere four decades elapsed between Cleisthenes and Ephialtes. For Rome the ancients themselves provided a location: in the fictitious reign of good king Servius and the era of the legendary Cincinnatus-at-the-plough. Plato, we remember, gave the short answer to all such rhetoric: in reply to those who contrasted the later 'demagogues' with the leaders of the good old days, he insisted that Miltiades and Themistocles were no better, that they were merely more accomplished in gratifying the desires of the *demos*, like pastrycooks and not like statesmen (*Gorgias* 502E–519D). But then, Plato was a consistent moralist, not a historian.

Yet the time came when serious politics disappeared from the Greek city-states and from Rome, and we have to ask why and how

[34] Astin (1968) 15.

that happened. There is no single answer. The typical Greek city-state was too small to hold out indefinitely against larger and stronger states, Athens, Sparta or Thebes in the classical period, then Macedon, the Seleucid and Attalid rulers, and finally Rome. What passed for politics in subject cities is, as I have already said, uninteresting. Those few that might have been worth examining cannot be studied for lack of evidence. I could add Rhodes to my earlier list because it remained fully independent until the middle of the second century B.C. and there are tantalizing hints in the literature of a genuine political life.[35] But we know nothing of it, though I cannot resist the temptation of recalling that Rhodes was a conquest-state, having acquired and retained important revenue-producing territory on neighbouring islands and on the mainland of Asia Minor.[36] Spartan politics after the defeat at Leuctra in 371 B.C. and the consequent loss of Messenia are even more elusive than for the previous period. Chapters have been written – there is sufficient source-material – about Spartan wars in the century after Leuctra, their activity as mercenaries as far afield as southern Italy, relations with Persia, conflicts within the Peloponnese, relations with the Achaean and Aetolian leagues, but in all this detail I can find virtually nothing about domestic affairs in Sparta other than personal quarrels among kings and a few other 'leaders' and indications of the catastrophic decline in manpower (full citizens were now being counted in three figures). Then, without warning to us, so to speak, came the explosions under Agis and Cleomenes and again under Nabis, and the significant point is that these kings actually attempted a complete redistribution of the land and possibly the export of their revolution.[37]

Only the Athenian evidence is, as usual, informative, and the conclusion is really quite simple. After the death of Alexander in 323 B.C., Athens was hopelessly entangled in the wars and political manoeuvres of his successors and would-be successors. *Stasis* became the rule: Antipater imposed an oligarchic system in 322, in

---

[35] See recently J. L. O'Neil, 'How Democratic was Hellenistic Rhodes?', *Athenaeum*, n.s. 59 (1981) 468–73.

[36] A warning is necessary against recent publications, based chiefly on Hellenistic epigraphic texts, that claim to be analysing government and politics but turn out to be no more than catalogues of official titles, speculation about governmental machinery, and miscellaneous legislative matters that happen to be recorded.

[37] See B. Shimron, *Late Sparta* (Arethusa Monographs 3, 1972); P. Oliva, *Sparta and Her Social Problems* (Prague 1971), part III.

318 Cassander installed Demetrius of Phalerum as tyrant, and after his overthrow there were seven changes of government between 307 and 261.[38] For two generations, in other words, there was still a remarkably strong drive to restore the old political way of life, and enough leaders willing to make a go of it. The old institutions and methods kept coming back to life. But superior power told: Macedonian garrisons in Athens and armies swirling about and in the area made the decisions in the end. Significantly, even when politics looked most 'normal' the various groupings were invariably identified by the Macedonian contenders for power with whom they were associated. After 261 B.C. Athens permanently entered the ranks of the subject city-states with paltry politics, the victim of superior external force.

Finally Rome. The last century of the Republic was filled with all the traditional political manifestations – electoral excitement, factional politics, laws and plebiscites. Yet a profound change set in with the massacre of Tiberius Gracchus and his followers in 133 B.C. I need only enumerate the most familiar subsequent outbursts: the bloodshed that brought down Gaius Gracchus in 121, the violence surrounding Saturninus in the years 103–100, the era of Sulla from his march on Rome in 88 to his abdication as dictator in 79, the conspiracy of Catiline in 63, the running gang warfare of Clodius and Milo between 58 and 52, the decades of the first triumvirate, Caesar and the civil war between Antony and the future Augustus.[39] Political conflict that is under permanent threat of massacres, proscriptions and invading armies (even though Roman, not foreign) – a threat that became a reality with growing frequency – ceases to be the politics which we have been studying.

If I am asked, as I have been, what difference there was between the 'gangs' of the first century B.C. and the 'mobs' that took to the streets in earlier centuries, my answer is that there was a fundamental qualitative distinction. Gangs of hired professional thugs became for the first time a permanent element of the political scene

[38] The fullest account remains that of Ferguson (1911) ch. 1–4. One should not be misled by Ferguson's title, 'Athens under Tory Democracy', for his chapter on second-century B.C. Athens.

[39] The chronological list in Lintott (1968) App. A, headed 'Acts of Violence in Rome', is too eccentric to be useful. It includes imprisonment of consuls by tribunes to prevent a military levy ('in effect formalized violence') and some individual assassinations along with the Catilinarian conspiracy, but not Caesar's crossing the Rubicon.

in Rome.[40] They and their paymasters had the will and the ability to employ armed force, of 'gangs' or legions or both together, in order to compel the governmental organs to take specified decisions. In the first generation after Tiberius Gracchus the practice was rather sporadic; thereafter it became the rule in the sense that everyone was aware of the threat and that those who possessed the power were quicker and quicker to turn the threat into a reality. That had never been the case in the Republic previously, and, though one may have difficulty in drawing sharp lines, I find it incomprehensible that a distinguished historian of Rome, in an influential work, *Party Politics in the Age of Caesar*, could reduce the reality to a bland sentence, 'Sometimes the generals used their personal armies for intimidation of voters.'[41] Constitutional precedents were the only argument Cicero could offer in support of the extraordinary commands voted to Pompey or of the triumvirate, but a modern historian is free, indeed obligated, not to play such charades. In reality, binding decisions were no longer reached by discussion and argument and ultimately by voting; often not even in appearance.

In one important respect, the change that came about during the last century of the Roman Republic was the last stage in a continuous development rather than a sudden breach with the past. Throughout the history of the city-state, Greek even more than Roman, rivalry within the political élite had an all-or-nothing quality: one sought not merely to overcome competitors for leadership but to destroy them, figuratively and sometimes literally. Ostracism was a symbol of the gentler form, the political trials the common manifestation of a more severe form, assassination the final form. To be sure, arrogant ruthlessness has been a characteristic of successful holders of power in all complex societies – 'après moi le déluge' is merely a *reductio ad absurdum*. Without the proper mixture of arrogance and ruthlessness no one could attain the highest power. Historians have their conventional scapegoats, Alcibiades, Tiberius Gracchus or Catiline, but I do not find their psychology to be essentially different from that of the 'heroes', Pericles or the two Catos.

That said, the critical questions still remain: Why in antiquity was it necessary to 'destroy' political opponents and not just their political positions? And why in the Roman Republic did the

---

[40] Lintott (1968) 74.   [41] Taylor (1949) 69.

practice turn into continued armed combat that brought an end to the system itself? In a few closing remarks I can do no more than offer some pointers. Central to both questions, I suggest, is *direct* popular participation in government (even as restricted as it was in Rome), an element that has been absent from all the subsequent history of politics, barring a few exceptions. No matter how closed and solidary the ruling class, its politically ambitious members were compelled to seek continuing support from the mass of the citizenry, and to undermine support for their rivals. In a world that clung to the face-to-face city-state community, no matter how fictitious it became in reality, the most effective way of accomplishing the latter was to break rivals, by moral obloquy, by financial penalties, and, best of all, by physically removing them from the community through exile or death. The combat was highly personal because of the constitutional and governmental machinery. Power did not rest on, or derive from, office or any other formal base. The forums in which it expressed itself constitutionally were large bodies, councils or assemblies, which met frequently and had few restraints on their right of decision-making; hence the continuous tension in the lives of the leaders. Hence, too, the necessity of building up a personal network, through family alliances and through all the possible forms of patronage. Close lieutenants and agents ran the same risks as their patrons and were often, indeed, the first victims. The mass of supporters ran few risks, other than disappointment, until civil war replaced politics.

To be sure, the ancients failed to make the necessary constitutional adjustments that would have permitted political parties to come into being, but that was not a 'cause' of breakdown. No constitutional system has ever prevented civil war and dissolution, and the question still remains: Why was there so little resistance in all sections of the Roman citizenry to the visible breakdown of the system? I stress 'so little resistance': the vast bulk of Cicero's writings only creates an illusion of effective (as distinct from intellectual) opposition within the élite.[42] The soldiers, commented Syme years ago, 'now recruited from the poorest classes in Italy,

---

[42] An interesting case has now been made that Cicero's bitterest enemy, Clodius (murdered in 52 B.C.), led a genuine and wholly exceptional movement of the urban poor and dispossessed: W. Nippel, 'Die *plebs urbana* und die Rolle der Gewalt in der späten römischen Republik', in *Vom Elend der Handarbeit*, ed. H. Mommsen & W. Schulze (Stuttgart 1981), pp. 70–92.

were ceasing to feel allegiance to the State; military service was for livelihood, or from constraint, not a natural and normal part of a citizen's duty'.[43] They were drawn from the peasantry, while the urban poor settled for bread and circuses, with cash on the side in bribes or in payment for a bit of thuggery. The majority, of course, struggled along on their farms or in their shops and in odd jobs as best they could, as they had done in an earlier age.

In other words, there was a widespread and fundamental change in attitudes with respect to the state. Most historians shy from psychological explanations of such change, partly from an understandable fear of the moralizing rhetoric that flows in their wake, partly from ignorance or distrust of social psychology, but largely because of hardened professional traditions. Yet it is an indubitable fact that for centuries the Roman state had been an exploitative instrument unique in antiquity in strength, brutality and the scale and reach of the exploitation. The preservation of the 'anachronistic' city-state structure, noticed by all historians, was not a mere technical flaw – the Principate also had no bureaucracy and was for a long time equally centred in Rome. More important, it seems to me, is the consequence that both control and the major benefits of exploitation were retained by a small circle. Given the Roman political system, continuous conquest increased the stakes and intensified the arrogant power drives of individual members of the élite, ultimately to the point that they were willing to march on Rome (whatever motives they may have imagined for themselves). Only a loss of imperial power might conceivably have checked this process, but it in fact continued to grow during the civil war: Sulla could take time off from his domestic concerns to defeat Mithridates, Caesar to conquer Gaul.

The mass of the citizenry shared in the exploitative psychology; that is to say, they also believed in the conqueror's right to spoils and, at different and descending levels, they obtained a portion. By the middle of the second century B.C., however, the costs were becoming visibly too disproportionate to the benefits. Military

---

[43] Syme (1939) 15. After 89 B.C. perhaps the majority of 'Romans' in the armies were Italians who had acquired Roman citizenship *en bloc* as a result of the Social War. I see no way to assess the relative importance of that phenomenon on the psychology of the army rank-and-file. After all, for perhaps two centuries Italian 'allies' had been conscripted into the Roman armies (and fought well) in a ratio that varied from one to two Italians for each Roman: see Brunt (1971*b*) 677–86; V. Ilari, *Gli Italici nelle strutture militari romane* (Milan 1974).

demands became more and more of a burden and from the end of the third century it became increasingly necessary to draw into the armies men who lacked the traditional property qualifications.[44] Colonization virtually ceased and when the Gracchan attempts to redistribute *ager publicus* failed, conquest ceased to be what Max Weber called 'purpose-rational' for the poorer classes. But the economic needs remained and so did the exploitative psychology, reinforced by the introduction of large-scale slavery into Italy (a subject I have been compelled to put aside in this book). Therefore, in the absence of a serious challenge to the traditional legitimacy of hierarchy (itself a question deserving extended analysis), Romans and Italians in their tens and hundreds of thousands turned to individuals to provide them with what the state had failed to offer. To repeat Syme's words, men 'were ceasing to feel allegiance to the state'; or in Weberian terms, conquest and the state itself were also no longer 'value-rational'. Roman armies marched against other Roman armies and against Rome itself as readily as against the armies of Mithridates. Politics had ceased to be instrumentally useful to the populace, and the ultimate solution proved to be the end not only of popular participation but of politics itself.

[44] See E. Gabba, *Republican Rome, the Army and the Allies*, trans. P. J. Cuff (Oxford 1976), ch. 1–2.

6

IDEOLOGY

In 415 B.C. the Athenians mounted a full-scale invasion of Sicily in a bold and imaginative effort to force a successful conclusion to the war against Sparta that had commenced more than fifteen years earlier. Not long after the landing in Sicily, Alcibiades, a moving spirit of the invasion scheme and one of the three generals in command, was summoned home to face charges of plotting to overthrow the democratic regime. He went into exile instead, was sentenced to death *in absentia*, and quickly made his way to Sparta. There he participated publicly in strategic discussions regarding the conduct of the war, excusing his turncoat behaviour in these words (according to Thucydides 6.92.4):

As for love of *polis*, I do not feel it for the one that is wronging me but for the one in which I safely exercised my rights as a citizen. I do not accept that I am marching against my fatherland; on the contrary, I seek to reconquer a fatherland that has ceased to be mine. It is genuine love of *polis* not when one refuses to march against it, having lost it unjustly, but when through the ardour of one's desire one tries all means to recover it.

The shabby, self-serving argument of a traitor? Certainly Alcibiades is one of the first names mentioned today whenever a politician or journalist wishes to display a bit of learning on the subject of treason, and historians, too, are usually satisfied with that quick dismissal. However, once we free ourselves from the emotionalism of the word 'treason', it should be clear that Alcibiades' self-defence (however we assess its strength or weakness) opens in an extreme case two central, interrelated questions: What gives a regime legitimacy? What are the nature, limits and warrant of political obligation? More concretely, why, apart from the threat of punishment, should a citizen accept as binding on him an order to go to war, to pay taxes, or to stand trial on a charge of blasphemy? These are difficult questions, not sufficiently answered by calling upon patriotism, for example, which is no more than a particular conception of the ground for obligation to the community. The Athenians themselves appear not to have found the Alcibiades affair so simple: he was recalled four years later to take charge of the war effort, and those who opposed this move failed to make much capital of his treason. And today we grant political asylum to Soviet dissidents or to Iranian refugees from the regime of the Ayatollah and we negotiate with or even finance governments in exile; we recognize the right of conscientious objection to military service, we examine the possible theoretical foundations of civil disobedience.[1] Political obligation is not open-ended: it is determined by the nature of the regime and by the areas in which it may 'legitimately' command.

It is indisputable that the stable Greek city-states and republican Rome retained widespread political allegiance for long periods of time. But that is a tautology. It is no less a fact that many city-states were unable to command sustained allegiance and went from *stasis* to *stasis*. This fact, along with the variety of governmental arrangements to be found within the Greek world, stimulated the first attempts in history at conscious political analysis and reflection, as we glimpse them from the middle of the fifth century B.C. in the Athenian drama, in the histories of Herodotus and Thucydides, in the pamphlet on the Athenian 'constitution' falsely attributed to Xenophon, and in fragments or quotations from the Sophists. How widely the discussion was engaged in throughout the hundreds of dispersed Greek communities cannot be determined from the very poor evidence available. There can be no doubt about Athens: there it was continuous, intense and *public*. However, it is symptomatic that not one of the major Sophists was an Athenian, that they originated and were active all over the Greek world (though they of course spent time in Athens), and that they were respected in their home cities and played a considerable role there. The taint that has been attached ever since to them and to the very word 'sophist' is an historical untruth for which Plato is responsible, with minor assistance from Aristophanes.[2]

Political reflection need not be systematic analysis, and rarely is.

---

[1] E.g. B. Zwiebach, *Civility and Disobedience* (Cambridge 1975); Peter Singer, *Democracy and Obedience* (Oxford 1973).

[2] See the brilliant reply to Plato by George Grote, *A History of Greece* VI (rev. ed., London 1862), pp. 51–98. The fullest, massively documented accounts of the Sophists are M. Untersteiner, *The Sophists*, trans. Kathleen Freeman (London 1957); W. Nestle, *Vom Mythos zum Logos* (2 ed., Stuttgart 1942), ch. 9 (nearly 200 pp., not critical enough of the late ancient sources).

In the realm of politics only Plato and Aristotle (and possibly as a transitional figure, the Sophist Protagoras) may properly be labelled systematic thinkers. They were the first genuine political theorists of antiquity, and the last; the first and last to attempt a complete and coherent account of the ideal organization of society grounded in systematic metaphysics, epistemology, psychology and ethics.[3] And both failed and admitted failure, Plato by writing the *Laws*,[4] Aristotle by the state in which he left the papers that were published more than three centuries later as the *Politics*, disorganized, digressive, incomplete, at times incoherent and inconsistent.[5] In the attempt, both Plato and Aristotle worked and wrote on a level of philosophical abstraction, sophistication and generalization that was not only beyond the reach of their fellow-men but was also unsuitable for the purposes of the present discussion. They do not and cannot tell us what Greeks generally understood by legitimacy, political obligation or proper political behaviour; they only tell us why the Greeks were held to have persistently and unavoidably misunderstood what they were doing and why they were doing it.

This is not to agree with two still persistently held notions, either that historians, pamphleteers and particularly playwrights (and their audiences) are not to be studied as thinkers at all; or that there was no bridge of any kind between them and the handful of

---

[3] 'No tutor would accept from a pupil the reasons given by Plato for the following quite important doctrines: that the Soul is tripartite; that if the Soul is tripartite, the ideal society would be a three-class state; that whatever exists, exists in order to perform one and only one function; that reason is one such function; that one and only one of the classes should be taught to reason; that membership of a class should normally be determined by pedigree; that empirical science can never be "real" science; that there are Forms; that only knowledge of Forms is "real" science; that only those who have this knowledge can have good political judgment; that political institutions must degenerate unless there are rulers who have had the sort of higher education that Plato describes; that "justice" consists in doing one's own job; and so on. Yet if any one of these propositions is dubitable, the positive recommendations of the "Republic" are unestablished': Gilbert Ryle, in a review of Karl Popper, *The Open Society and Its Enemies*, in *Mind* 56 (1947) 167–72, at pp. 169–70; reprinted in *Plato, Popper and Politics*, ed. R. Bambrough (Cambridge and New York, 1967), pp. 85–90.

[4] 'No serious reader of the *Laws* could reasonably doubt that Plato wrote into it, without the slightest hedging, propositions which contradict the very tenets I have presented . . . as indispensable supports of his meta-normative theory of justice . . . Though he does not discuss the earlier theory, does not allude to it in any way, we can be certain he has abandoned it': Vlastos (1977) 35–7.

[5] For an introduction to the complex story of the publication of Aristotle's works, see I. Düring, *Aristoteles* (Heidelberg 1966), pp. 32–52.

'rational' theorists and philosophers.[6] As MacIntyre has phrased it strikingly,

The Athenians had not insulated, as we have by a set of institutional devices, the pursuit of political ends from dramatic representation or the asking of philosophical questions from either. Hence we lack, as they did not, *any* public, generally shared communal mode either for representing political conflict or for putting our politics to the philosophical question.[7]

Can one imagine that of the ten or twelve or fourteen thousand who were present at the performance of Sophocles' *Antigone* in about 442 B.C., only a few philosophers understood that, among other things, the play raised the question of legitimacy and political obligation? Or that the audience were so busy laughing all through the *Acharnians* of Aristophanes, produced when the war against Sparta was already in its sixth year, that no one noticed that the resolution was a private peace made with Sparta by an old Athenian farmer, or that his name was Dicaeopolis, which means just (or righteous) *polis*? Or that only modern scholars have caught the intended answer to Socrates' doctrine – no one does evil knowingly – in the soliloquy of Euripides' *Medea* before she kills her children (lines 1078–80), 'I know what evil I am about to do; but the *thymos* is stronger than my resolution, *thymos*, the root of man's most evil acts' (where *thymos* is her irrational self)?

Not all Athenians held the same views and not all Greeks were Athenians, but the evidence is decisive that nearly all of them would have accepted as premises, one might say as axioms, that the good life was possible only in a *polis*, that the good man was more or less synonymous with the good citizen, that slaves, women and barbarians were inferior by nature and so excluded from all discussion; that therefore correct political judgments, the choice between *polis* regimes or between conflicting policies within a particular *polis*, should be determined by which alternative helped advance the good life. The main divergences were in practical judgments, not in the

---

[6] As a corrective, see the review-article by A. W. H. Adkins, 'Problems in Greek Popular Morality', *Classical Philology* 73 (1978) 143–58.

[7] MacIntyre (1981) 129–30. However, such public discussion did not lead to the formulation of a democratic *political theory* beyond that of Protagoras. It is a fallacy to think that there had to be one; or that its absence is seriously puzzling (so N. Loraux, *L'invention d'Athènes* (Paris 1981), pp. 176–85); or that it is possible to reconstruct one, as A. H. M. Jones tried to do in *Athenian Democracy* (Oxford 1957), ch. 3.

premises. Both Plato and Aristotle shared the premises,[8] which, it is worth stressing, they made no serious attempt to prove, but they embedded them in an over-arching scheme of human nature and human life that logically compelled them to challenge current political judgments, in Plato's case to reject them *all* as false. Aristotle admittedly presents a more variegated approach: his 'empiricism' and his powerful sociological bent constantly distract him from ideal (or Vlastos' 'meta-normative'[9]) considerations to normative judgments of current practices and beliefs. He could not, for instance, resist the temptation to teach even tyrants and oligarchs how to go about their business more successfully. It therefore appears that Aristotle the sociologist, if not Aristotle the philosopher, offers brilliant insights into existing Greek political views. And so he does, as in the stress on class that we considered in the first chapter. However, the sociologist and the philosopher were not two distinct *personae* who refrained from communicating with each other.[10] In the area of our immediate concern such a false division has the consequence that arguments from selected bits of Aristotle to political realities, and vice versa, turn out to be circular on too many important questions when external controls are lacking.[11]

So far I have been considering Greeks only, for the simple reason that with respect to political reflection and discussion, the difference between Greeks and Romans was about as wide as it is possible to be. One can with complete accuracy repeat my earlier quotation from MacIntyre, merely replacing 'we' by 'the Romans': they lacked any public, generally shared communal mode either for representing political conflict or for putting their politics to the philosophical question.[12] None of the vehicles for political reflec-

---

[8] For an excellent succinct statement, see MacIntyre (1981) ch. 11: 'The Virtues at Athens'.   [9] Vlastos (1977) 11.

[10] The classic exposure of this type of fallacy with respect to Aristotle's logic and metaphysics is G. E. L. Owen, 'The Platonism of Aristotle', *Proceedings of the British Academy* 50 (1965) 125–50, reprinted in *Articles on Aristotle*, ed. J. Barnes et al., 1 (London 1975), pp. 14–34.

[11] The whole of Part 1 of Nippel (1980) may be read as a demonstration of this point. It is perhaps also worth dismissing efforts to argue from the notorious affinity with tyrants of alleged pupils of Plato and Aristotle, most notably Demetrius of Phalerum, on whom see now Gehrke (1978); and of course from the fable that Plato hoped to introduce his ideal state in Syracuse through the agency of the drunken tyrant Dionysius II and the adventurer Dio, on which see Finley (1979) ch. 7.

[12] For what follows immediately, see the fine summary by Meyer (1961) 251–4.

tion that we enumerated in fifth-century Athens existed in Roman society. Roman dramatists, notably, were men of low social status who rarely dared jibe at important public figures and never discussed fundamental questions of political institutions or obligations.[13] For political speculation we have to come down as late as Polybius, and it is decisive that he was a Greek writing for Greeks in the mid-second century B.C. The theme of his *History* is stated at the outset (1.1.5): 'How and under what type of "constitution"' were the Romans able to subjugate most of the inhabited world in half a century? That was a Greek question, not a Roman one, and Polybius sought the answer in Greek constitutional history and theory, where there was in fact no answer suitable to Rome. So Polybius fell back on the 'mixed constitution', which never existed in reality. In a few pages of Book VI he produced a mish-mash of pseudo-theoretical and partly incompatible notions learned in the Hellenistic schools of rhetoric in which scions of the ruling class in the Achaean League were educated. The upshot was that to fit Rome (which also had no mixed constitution) into the scheme, Polybius could not give an accurate picture of the Roman governmental structure: his pretentious but shallow speculative analysis 'blinded him, to an extraordinary degree, to the elaborate texture of political life which throughout this period ensured the domination of the *nobiles*'.[14]

Polybius' 'philosophical' views were without any influence or even resonance among contemporary Romans. There is a tenacious fiction that an intellectual 'circle' gravitating round Scipio Aemilianus undertook to imbue the *nobilitas* with Stoic ideas of *humanitas* and natural law, under the immediate influence of the philosopher Panaetius of Rhodes, but it has been irrefutably demonstrated that this 'circle' was an invention of Cicero's.[15] When Cicero composed his *Republic* between 54 and 51 B.C., the long débâcle

[13] See H. D. Jocelyn, 'The Poet Cn. Naevius, P. Cornelius Scipio and Q. Caecilius Metellus', *Antichthon* 3 (1969) 32–47.
[14] F. W. Walbank, *Polybius* (Berkeley 1972), p. 155. This judgment is notable because Walbank rates Polybius far higher as a thinker than I do. The best recent assessment of Polybius' mixed constitution will be found in Nippel (1980) 142–53.
[15] H. Strasburger, 'Der "Scipionenkreis"', *Hermes* 94 (1966) 60–72, reprinted in Strasburger (1982) II 946–58. For a cool account of the Roman interest in Greek philosophy more generally, see H. D. Jocelyn, 'The Ruling Class of the Roman Republic and Greek Philosophers', *Bulletin of the John Rylands Library* 59 (1977) 323–66.

IDEOLOGY

that brought an end to the Roman city-state was in its final decade. Cicero located the 'dialogue' in 129 B.C., thus signalling his gloomy assessment of the current state of the *res publica*; and he chose as the main protagonists the famous general Scipio Aemilianus and his rather insignificant associate Laelius, signalling the view that is stated explicitly more than once in the work, namely, that what an experienced Roman statesman has to say is 'much more fruitful than the whole body of Greek writings' (1.23.37). So much for philosophers, whom Cicero, unlike Polybius, had read, including Plato after whom he allegedly modelled both the *Republic* and the companion work, the *Laws*. Like Mommsen, I find the central idea of the *Republic* 'as unphilosophical as unhistorical'[16] and I am not persuaded otherwise by the unending flood of adulatory commentaries.[17] Both works are filled with valuable explanations of the working and the 'spirit' of the Roman political system, notably of the ways by which the plebs were held so completely in check (a feature that Polybius had ignored completely). But of 'metanormative' analysis there is none; there is only rhetoric, in which I include the Stoic notions of 'natural law' and 'natural reason' that have loomed so large in western writing from the Church Fathers to our own day. Whatever genuinely philosophical meaning those terms may have had for the Stoics themselves, Cicero turned them into mere rhetoric, terms of 'approval for whatever idea (one) wanted to recommend at any particular time',[18] in his case the Roman constitution of the good old days.

On any assessment of Cicero, in the end the capital fact remains that the Romans had to wait for him and his younger contemporary, the historian Sallust, to offer *Roman* political reflection of the sort the Greeks had been familiar with from the fifth century B.C. Even though we concede the possibility that earlier examples have been lost, in the speeches of Cato or of Tiberius Gracchus, for instance, the fundamental contrast between the two societies

[16] T. Mommsen, *The History of Rome*, trans. W. P. Dickson (London 1908), v 508 (= III 622 in the standard German ed.).
[17] As an extreme illustration of the nonsense Cicero continues to evoke, I submit the still regularly cited book by V. Pöschl, *Römischer Staat und griechisches Staatsdenken bei Cicero* (Berlin 1936), which concludes (p. 173) that the *Republic* 'fused into one the Roman empire, perhaps the greatest creation of that world, and the philosophy of Plato, the most sublime spiritual creation of antiquity'.
[18] G. Watson, 'The Natural Law and Stoicism', in *Problems in Stoicism*, ed. A. A. Long (London 1971), pp. 216–38, at p. 235.

remains.[19] Some explanation is required, and immediately we observe the absence in Rome of the two stimuli initiating Greek political reflection we noticed earlier. The Romans were not faced with the puzzle of the great variety in constitutional arrangements that characterized the classical Greek world. There may have been variety within Italy, but the sole Roman concern with their neighbours (in and out of Italy) was to conquer them. This they did with calculated ferocity accompanied by contempt.[20] There was nothing requiring analysis or explanation. Secondly, the severe *stasis* of the early history of the Roman Republic was a conflict provoked by plebeian demands for concessions, not a civil war over alternative forms of government. Hence the Romans had no experience of the 'cycle of constitutions', not even of the choice between democracy and oligarchy or of the menace of tyranny (except on the part of Etruscan kings whom they had overthrown early on), two themes that dominated Greek political writing but made no appearance among Roman writers.

One other distinction merits consideration. Stress has been placed earlier on the citizen–soldier link and on the 'normality' of war in the city-state, both Greek and Roman. However, there were differences that gave the behaviour of the Romans, and particularly their psychology, a quality, or at least a nuance, setting them apart from the Greeks (most markedly from Athens, least so from Sparta). In the first place, the regularity, scale, duration, and geographical spread of Roman campaigning were incomparable with Greek practice, and the differences were steadily magnified as the Romans moved relentlessly from subjugating their neighbours to the conquest of Italy and then of the inhabited world. Secondly, the Roman citizen-militia was totally integrated into the hierarchical structure of society, as the Athenian was not. It is necessary only to recall that command of the armies was automatically the duty of the consuls (or their surrogates when required), so that 'consul' and 'general' were synonyms, as was not the case in Greece, and the consul-generals had *imperium*, a power with sacral overtones that

---

[19] In the case of Cato, there is good enough reason to accept Plutarch's summary (*Cato* 23.1) that he was hostile to philosophy and philosophers in general, and to Socrates in particular: the latter sought 'to be tyrant of his fatherland, overthrowing its customs and diverting its citizens to opinions contrary to the laws'. Cato is therefore most unlikely to have constituted an exception; see Astin (1978) ch. 8, 10. [20] See Harris (1979) 50–3.

Polybius could not express because he had no Greek word that was suitable.[21] And thirdly, *imperium* was but one expression of the central place of war in the religion, including the formal ritual system, of the Roman state.[22] Of course the Greeks also began and conducted wars with appeals to the gods and with thanksgiving at the end, but the Greek sacral calendar lacked the series of military festivals that filled the pontifical Roman calendar for the whole of the campaigning season, and their war-god Ares had virtually no cults in contrast to the very powerful and constantly worshipped Mars.[23] Nor was there a Greek parallel to the *sacramentum*, a particularly solemn oath of loyalty to his general that every Roman soldier and officer swore each time he was called up and which he was required to repeat whenever the general was changed.[24]

All this encourages me to believe that obedience to the authorities became so deeply embedded in the psyche of the ordinary Roman citizen that it carried over into his explicitly political behaviour. As with the Spartans, that fortified acceptance of the system to the degree that there was no genuine political discussion (as distinct from disagreements over specific policies directly affecting class interests). I find it inconceivable, for example, that a citizen of Athens or of many other Greek city-states would have allowed the *senatus consultum ultimum* to be introduced by the Senate without any serious challenge, and certainly no fundamental challenge, to its legitimacy.

And so we are wholly in the realm of ideology, not of political theory or philosophy (hence the title of this chapter); precisely the beliefs and attitudes that the few genuine theorists usually rejected. We are also in the realm of constant change, variation and imprecision. There were fundamental differences in political ideology between Greeks and Romans; among both between the archaic age and the developed 'classical' period; among the Greeks, between

---

[21] See the final pp. of ch. 3 above.

[22] H. Le Bonniec, 'Aspects religieux de la guerre à Rome', in *Problèmes de la guerre à Rome*, ed. J.-P. Brisson (Paris and The Hague 1969), pp. 101–15.

[23] Pritchett (1971–9) III 154–63.

[24] Any supposed parallel with the 'ephebic oath' in Athens is essentially false. Once in his life, on coming of military age, a young man swore a generalized oath of loyalty to the community, not of loyalty to an individual general. Text and translation of the oath are given, with a brief commentary, in C. Pélékidis, *Histoire de l'éphébie attique* (Paris 1962), pp. 110–13.

Athens and Sparta, between oligarchies and democracies, between states with more and states with less popular participation. Analysis is further complicated by the ways in which a small number of words and phrases were rhetorically deployed with different nuances and sometimes with divergent and even contradictory meanings. For instance, *eunomia*, a favourite word in Greek ideological debates, had the root-sense of 'good order', 'concord', then became a standard aristocratic slogan which democratic spokesmen in turn refused to surrender to their opponents.[25] Sometimes the sense in any given passage is obvious, but often it can be discovered only by a close consideration of the speaker's outlook and orientation and of the specific context. And of course the same is true of the Greek and Latin words we translate as 'ancestral custom', 'freedom', 'commonwealth' (*res publica*) and so on through the whole political vocabulary.

Nevertheless, there was broad agreement on a few generalizations (beyond the premises already noticed about the *polis* and the good life). The first is in fact a negative one: the absence of any need to grapple with the problem of legitimacy, which today 'figures at the very heart of our concern with the nature and value of modern society' as 'a main dimension of *political culture*'.[26] It is not at all obvious why a problem that came to the fore in the Middle Ages and has been important ever since should not have arisen in antiquity, and I have no explanation to offer. The suggestion that its appearance in the Middle Ages was 'prompted by the collapse of direct rule in the ancient world' does not convince:[27] why did the transformation of Athenian government by Cleisthenes, the persistence of oligarchy, the acceptance by Greek city-states of the overlordship of Hellenistic monarchs and later of Rome, the overriding power of the Roman Senate and higher magistrates, or

---

[25] The variations are examined in detail in Grossmann (1950) ch. 2.

[26] Merquior (1980) 1. I shall be concerned solely with legitimacy in the specific sense of the title of a given political system to rule, not with the legitimacy of a particular dynasty or of a state in its foreign relations. Perhaps I should also say that 'legitimacy' is not a synonym of 'legality', though the two terms are etymologically linked and may overlap; they are also too often confused: see the symposium volume, *L'idée de légitimité* (Annales de philosophie politique 7, Paris 1967).

[27] Merquior (1980) 2, who follows R. Polin in the symposium cited in n. 26. Polin asserts the view without argument (pp. 17–18) and, in my judgment, proceeds to undermine it in the succeeding few pages.

the creation of a monarchy by Augustus not prompt comparable discussion of the title to rule? Not that there was not discussion enough, but it cannot be seriously held that Augustus' claim to have restored the *res publica*, for example, or the scattered juristic statements resting imperial authority on a grant by the 'senate and people'[28] are on the same level of discourse as the line of doctrines that stretches from William of Occam through Bodin, Hobbes, Locke, Rousseau to, say, Rawls.

What was discussed seriously from a relatively early date was the nature of justice. A proper state was an instrument of justice, and states were accordingly evaluated in terms of good or bad, better or worse, not (except rather casually in the case of tyranny) of legitimate or illegitimate. At an abstract level, notably with the Sophists, distinctions were drawn between the necessary ('natural') elements (*physis*) and the contingent (*nomos*) and there are disagreements over the advantages of one or the other in the state machinery. However, even those Sophists who formulated an embryonic contract theory – the law results from an agreement (or conspiracy) among the weak to curb the 'natural' power of the strong – offered no title to rule, no concept of legitimacy, for one governmental system in preference to another. Nor did Aristotle, while Plato, of course, demonstrated that all existing systems are necessarily illegitimate. Religion was pervasively in the background, but, as we have seen earlier, it made no contribution to specific legitimation. Justice came from the gods and they endowed man with reason and the potential to discriminate morally and therefore politically. But neither Greek nor Roman religion had the substantive doctrines or the ecclesiastical machinery to sanction (or legitimate) a particular ruler, regime or system. Lawgivers, rhetoricians and ideologists all spoke in the name of justice, but I am unaware of a single claim to divine sanction for a particular measure, regime, reform or revolution. There was no divine right, no theodicy in the Graeco-Roman world before the triumph of Christianity. Not even the Ptolemies, who were literally worshipped, nor the pagan Roman emperors, whose cult was not so simple and direct but a cult nonetheless, ever issued an edict as a divine command.

---

[28] See the detailed presentation by P. A. Brunt, 'Lex de imperio Vespasiani', *Journal of Roman Studies* 67 (1977) 95–116.

In more modern times, even kings claiming divine right were no
less insistent (when they had some basis, however thin) on the long
duration of their dynastic line: legitimacy 'consecrated by time' was
often a more powerful ideology than consecration by God in the
face of competing dynastic claims or revolutionary threats.[29] In
antiquity as throughout history, appeal to the past was usually a
conservative argument against fundamental change, or, as in Athens
in 411 B.C., for a backward change.[30] As with *eunomia*, however,
their political opponents could not leave to the 'aristocrats' so
strong an ideological weapon – the example of Demosthenes is
sufficient.[31] Neither side was concerned with historical accuracy;
they sought a 'usable' past, even if it had to be invented. It is
noteworthy how many of the greatest local heroes – Lycurgus in
Sparta, Theseus in Athens, Romulus in Rome – were purely
legendary figures. Direct evidence is lacking with which to measure
the appeal of constant stress on the great antiquity of a system
as a whole or of particular customs, institutions and practices.
However, there is more than sufficient evidence from later eras,
down to our own day, to suggest that the psychological impact was a powerful one. Continuity in time helped consecrate
'national' identity, and therefore identification with the system,
a sense of common involvement, belief in the legitimacy of the
regime.

An effective belief in legitimacy cannot, of course, be guaranteed
by long continuity in time alone, whether real or fictitious. Cicero's
desperate attempt in the *Republic* to keep the link alive was futile:
the system was no longer 'purpose-rational' (the Weberian phrase I
have used previously). It was as true of the ancient city-state as it is
in our world that among the citizenry at large there prevailed 'a
broadly utilitarian consensus that political obligation is owed (and
only owed) to political forms towards which it is to the long term
collective advantage to acknowledge it'.[32] How difficult it was for
the Greek *poleis* to maintain this consensus is immediately revealed
by the frequency of *stasis*. Why? The only answer I can offer is one I

[29] P. Bastid, p. 5 in the symposium volume cited in n. 26.
[30] See Finley (1975) ch. 2.
[31] See the Demosthenic material collected by F. Jost, *Das Beispiel und Vorbild der
Vorfahren* . . . (Paderborn 1935; repr. New York 1979), ch. 5; cf. more generally
L. Pearson, 'Historical Allusions in the Attic Orators', *Classical Philology* 36
(1941) 209–29. [32] Dunn (1980) 202.

have given repeatedly, that under ancient city-state conditions conquest alone made possible political stability, and therefore a utilitarian consensus. Rome was the quintessential case; hence after the archaic 'struggle of the orders' there was no serious *stasis* until the final period of the Republic that began with the Gracchi. Throughout the history of *stasis*, legitimacy was not proclaimed in justification by the rebels nor was a right of rebellion or even of disobedience formulated in general terms. Alcibiades' defence of his behaviour was a rare, if not unique, exception. *Stasis* was avowedly a clash of interests, nothing more, whether or not it was covered by rhetoric about justice or about 'true' equality.

Political obligation, a corollary of legitimacy, was also examined in antiquity in the most casual way, when it was not simply taken for granted, again in marked contrast to its central position in modern political thought from the late Middle Ages.[33] The commands of the magistrates 'shall be just and the citizens shall obey them willingly and without demur' (Cicero, *Laws* 3.3.6), is not followed by any consideration of the moral consequences if a magisterial command should be unjust. Underpinning the 'law' is Cicero's earlier exposition of the doctrine that *imperium* in the Roman style is the essential condition for a well-ordered state, for what the Greeks called *eunomia*. That is all, but not even Pericles' Funeral Oration, with its wonderful rhetoric about the superiority of Athens and its institutions, can add any more to what we might call a utilitarian argument than the brief, unexpected statement that 'fear' above all restrains us from acting illegally in the public domain (Thucydides 2.37.3).[34] Fear, however, helps explain political alle-

---

[33] Modern theorizing has proved to be inconclusive and often weak – sufficient bibliography will be found in Dunn (1980) – but that demonstrates the complexity of the concept, not its unimportance. The same can be said of legitimacy, but the only explanation of Bleicken's false conclusion in a three-page footnote (beginning on p. 92) that 'modern doctrines of the state and constitution now generally give up use of the concept of legitimacy' is that for him 'modern' is exclusively German, and more narrowly German political analysis with an anti-Weberism stance: J. Bleicken, *Staatliche Ordnung und Freiheit in der römischen Republik* (Frankfurter Althistorische Studien 6, 1972).

[34] I do not believe that Thucydides' choice of the rarer *deos* for 'fear' rather than the more common *phobos* suggests the nuance attested only in poetry, 'reverent fear', as does A. W. Gomme in his commentary, who finds 'no difficulty' in then translating *deos* here simply as 'respect'. The embarrassment of many modern commentators would be dissipated if they accepted the far from impossible view that the wording is Thucydides', not Pericles'.

giance, not political obligation.[35] (Military obligation was of course susceptible to more and different rhetoric, in terms of glory and defence of the community, in the Funeral Oration as in endless pages of Livy.)

The one exception, the only surviving attempt known to me of an *argument* to justify political obligation, appears in an unexpected place, in Plato's *Crito*, a brief early dialogue.[36] Socrates in prison, awaiting execution, firmly rejects the offer of his friends to procure his escape. His argument, in brief, is a minimally contractarian one: any man who has chosen throughout all his long life to remain a resident and citizen, and who, furthermore, has served on the Council and has carried out his military duties, has thereby agreed to obey the law and the decisions of legitimate authorities. Therefore an act of disobedience, even when the decision was an unjust one, would be morally wrong. There are insuperable difficulties: the argument contradicts the view Plato has Socrates express in the *Apology* (37E–38A); it is incompatible with everything Plato himself believed; it can be controverted as an argument without any reference to its historicity.[37] Despite all that, the text of the *Crito* exists, and its very exceptionalism tells us enough about the low ranking of political obligation (and also of civil disobedience) among explicit ideological concerns and disputes in antiquity.

Behind the argument of the *Crito* there lurked another proposition, that, in contrast, was endlessly restated and almost universally believed by city-state Greeks and Romans alike, even by Plato and Aristotle:[38] the essential condition for a genuine political society, for a true *polis* and therefore for the good life, is 'Rule by laws, not

---

[35] It is important to recognize the distinction between allegiance, a 'social fact', and obligation, an 'ideological category': Dunn (1980) 157.

[36] In saying that, I have not forgotten the jejune 'dialogue' between Socrates and Hippias in Xenophon's *Memorabilia* (4.4.12–25), to which credence is incomprehensibly given by modern scholars. The slippery Xenophon, whose philosophical pretensions far outran his capacities, clinched the claim that 'the lawful' (*to nomimon*) is also 'the just' (*to dikaion*) by citing the divine 'unwritten laws' requiring men to honour their parents and to abstain from sexual intercourse with them.

[37] The most elaborate analysis, uneven in quality and cogency, of the 'interesting bad argument' is that of A. D. Woozley, *Law and Obedience: The Arguments of Plato's Crito* (London 1979). A short preliminary account appeared some years earlier: 'Socrates on Disobeying the Law', in *The Philosophy of Socrates*, ed. G. Vlastos (Garden City, N.Y., 1971), pp. 299–318.

[38] E.g. *Republic* 565E–566A; *Politics* 1295a19–23.

by men.' Democracy and oligarchy shared that claim to virtue;[39] so did the legendary archaic monarchy retrospectively after it had been endowed in later times with a full panoply of institutions. Innumerable statements of the slogan can be quoted down to Cicero in the last days of the Roman Republic. One will suffice, from *The Suppliant Women* of Euripides (lines 312–13): 'The power that keeps cities of men together is noble preservation of the laws.' Modern analytical philosophers have no difficulty in dismissing the slogan as uselessly vague and woolly, but they are misdirecting their effort: ideology is not theory and should not be subjected to the same sort of rigorous analysis. The test of ideology is pragmatic, not logical; in antiquity that meant stability, the ability to avoid frequent *stasis* and particularly *stasis* in its extreme form of civil war. It was not mere woolliness to have insisted on, and even fought for, written laws and law codes in the archaic days of aristocratic rule. The judgment that demanded fixed, publicly known laws was sound, the reasoning eminently practical.

A bit later in *The Suppliant Women* a herald arrives in Athens from Thebes and asks, 'Who is ruler (*tyrannos*) of this land?' King Theseus retorts, 'Your start was wrong, stranger, seeking a *tyrannos* here. This city is free and ruled by no one man. The *demos* reigns, taking turns annually. They do not give supremacy to the rich; the poor man has an equal share in it.' That's mob rule, replies the herald: 'The *demos* is not right judge of arguments; then how can it give right guidance to the city?'[40] But he did not challenge the principle of rule of law. The disagreement was over who formulated the laws that then bound everyone, rulers and ruled alike. There lay the great divide among ancient city-states, in their forms of government and therefore in the shape and direction of their politics; between oligarchies and democracies, of course, but more precisely, as the case of Rome shows, according to the formal extent and real effectiveness of popular participation in government and politics.

That divide, over who in principle shared in the law-making

---

[39] The denial by Demosthenes (24.75–6) and Aeschines (3.6) that oligarchies were ruled by law merely reveals that truth was not a necessary condition in political oratory.

[40] *Suppliant Women* 399–419 (translated by Frank Jones, with modifications). The elevation of Theseus in the early fifth century B.C. to be patron-saint of Athenian democracy is remarkable but irrelevant in the present discussion.

machinery, manifested itself in a cluster of political terms and phrases. Aristotle opened the *Politics* with a polemic against those who held that the 'statesman' was merely the master of slaves or the head of a household writ large. Not so, he argued, because the statesman 'rules and is ruled in turn'; that is natural, he said later on in the book, when the citizens are 'equals and peers' (1279a8–11). To the Athenian claim that they had achieved this state of affairs most completely because the *demos*, all the citizens, were equals and peers and therefore they all ruled and were ruled in turn, Aristotle's answer was that democratic procedure of this type rested on a false, arithmetical conception of equality, mere counting of heads, which eventually put control into the hands of demagogues who soon brought about the worst possible condition, rule by men, not by laws.[41] Plato agreed at length (*Republic* 562D–566C), but, unlike Aristotle, he did not believe that any other conception of equality could save the principle of ruling and being ruled in turn.

Cicero, in a brief flamboyant digression in one of his orations (*For Flaccus* 7.15–16), denounced the Athenians and the Greeks generally for thereby having turned genuine liberty into licence. Yet he himself had no difficulty in approving the principle for Rome (*Laws* 3.2.5) because under the Roman system the reference could only be to the higher magistracies, shared out annually among the *nobiles* and their occasional protégés of less distinguished ancestry. We know about this continuing and unresolvable ideological disagreement from the more reflective writers, but the heat and tenacity with which conflicting views were expressed suggests that there were resonances among the less articulate and the inarticulate. The reality that any Athenian could attend the Assembly, sit on the courts and the Council, and hold many of the offices could not have been without psychological impact;[42] nor could the reality that Roman aristocrats alone could rule as well as be ruled.

Central to all these divergences and disputes were the conflicting evaluations of the moral and intellectual qualities of whole classes and conditions of men, specifically of classes of citizens. A deeply

---

[41] Aristotle returned to the question often and in different contexts, so that a particular reference would be misleading. The passage on demagogues and their consequences is *Politics* 1292a1–36.

[42] I ignore here the limitation that a few high offices were barred to the majority of Athenians by property qualifications.

hierarchical valuation was explicit enough in the Theban messenger's reply to Theseus, more metaphorical but no less open in the varied vocabulary for 'rich' and 'poor' we considered in the opening pages of this book. If the *demos* is 'no right judge of arguments' (in Euripidean language), or, in Cicero's more colourful rhetoric, it is made up of 'men inexperienced in all matters, ignorant, untaught', 'artisans and shopkeepers and all such dregs of a city',[43] the conclusion seems indisputable that it does not qualify to share in the political decision-making. The issue however was complicated among both Greeks and Romans by the presence of large numbers of men who, whatever their personal qualities, were ranked below Cicero's dregs by their legal status as slaves. The contrary of 'slave' is 'free man' and even a Cicero conceded that all citizens shared the quality of freedom (as they also shared membership in the *polis*-community unlike the free non-citizens who resided in it, a feature of city-state life that need not concern us in the present context).

All city-states firmly acknowledged that all citizens were free (barring miscreants who had lost all or part of their freedom for one reason or another). That tells us something, but not enough. It is a commonplace that the actual content of 'freedom' varies greatly from time to time and from place to place – I do not propose to pursue that here, apart from the minimal aspect of freedom ('equality before the law') that is pertinent in the present context.[44] Most, if not all, city-states formally accepted that principle in the private sphere, that is to say, in all personal relations between individuals that could be actionable at law, and even in such relations between an individual and the state as were subject to judicial decision in case of dispute.[45] That such formal equality has never been achieved in practice wherever there is inequality in wealth, social connections, political authority is another commonplace. What matters here is the correlation between the extent of equality before the law and the extent of popular participation in government and politics (especially, though not only, in mem-

---

[43] Cicero, *Oration for Flaccus* 7.16; 8.18. The passage contains more such invective that I have not quoted.

[44] In particular I do not consider the peculiar and narrow conceptual range of political *libertas* in Rome, on which see Ch. Wirszubski, *Libertas as a Political Idea at Rome* . . . (Cambridge 1950), esp. pp. 13–15, immediately relevant in our context.

[45] On what follows immediately, see Finley (1976a).

bership on juries and other judicial organs). 'There is no true security for juristic liberty', wrote the English Hegelian, Bernard Bosanquet, 'apart from political liberty; and it has constantly been the infraction of juristic liberty that has been the origin of the demand for a share in highly positive political duties and functions.'[46]

In antiquity it was of course the Athenians who best exemplified that proposition. For them (and presumably for smaller democracies on the Athenian model), *isonomia*, the word we translate as 'equality before the law', came also to mean equality through the law; that is, equality among all the citizens in their political rights, an equality that was created by constitutional developments, by law. That equality meant not only the right to vote, to hold office, and so on, but above all the right to participate in policy-making in the Council and the Assembly. Debates in the Assembly were opened by the herald with these words, 'What man has good advice to give the *polis* and wishes to make it known?' That, said Theseus, is freedom (*Suppliant Women* 438–41). Protagoras explained the rationale: 'when the subject of their deliberation involves political wisdom . . . they listen to every man, for they think that everyone must share in this virtue; otherwise there could be no *polis*' (Plato, *Protagoras* 322E–323A). An appropriate Greek word was even coined in the early fifth century B.C., *isegoria*, meaning freedom of speech not so much with our conventional negative tone of freedom from censorship as in the more significant sense of right to speak out where it mattered most, in the assembly of all the citizens. There was no equivalent word in Latin because the only Roman parallel was the (at least formal) equality and freedom among the *nobiles*. In Rome, Momigliano has commented, 'one senses that freedom of speech belongs to the sphere of *auctoritas* just as much as to the sphere of *libertas*'.[47]

The Protagorean doctrine, if we may call it that, did not extend to the claim that everyone shared the 'virtue' of political wisdom in equal measure. The evidence strongly suggests that even in Athens few exercised their right of *isegoria*, and demonstrates beyond any

[46] B. Bosanquet, *The Philosophical Theory of the State* (4 ed., London 1923; orig. published 1899), pp. 127–8 of the paperback ed. (1965).
[47] A. D. Momigliano, 'Freedom of Speech in Antiquity', in *Dictionary of the History of Ideas* 2 (1973) 252–63, at p. 261. The contrast between Athenian and Roman theatre, already discussed, is related.

doubt that political leadership was monopolized by a relatively small stratum though not a self-perpetuating one as in Rome. The limit of universal political virtue was the universal right to share in the final decision on an equal, one-man-one-vote basis. Beyond that, the principle of inequality, of hierarchy, operated. Ironically, the consequence was that over two or more centuries, Athens had proportionately fewer incompetent generals and political spokesmen than Rome with its self-perpetuating élite and its annual turnover at the highest level, the consuls and praetors. Within the Senate the incompetents no doubt carried little influence, but they were plenipotentiary in the field and nearly so in their actions at home, armed as they were with *imperium*.

The fact – and I insist that it is a fact – that the Athenian *demos* displayed so much good discrimination in their selection of leaders, by vote in the case of the *strategoi* or by their support for individual policy-makers in the Assembly, cannot be explained by apathy, the favourite concept of our modern élitist school of political scientists. Apathy cannot be attributed to the many thousands who attended Assembly meetings with some frequency, who served on the Council once or twice, and who made up the jury-courts, again in the thousands. The only alternative, it seems to me, is to think of widespread civic responsibility, a moral attribute that historians seem to shy away from, understandably in part (but only in part) because of its evident subjectivity as a category and the difficulty in demonstrating its presence. It is so much easier to seize on a few instances of seemingly irresponsible behaviour, such as the execution on instruction of the Assembly of the generals who had commanded the victorious Athenian fleet at Arginusae in 406 B.C., as ground for condemnation of the system as a whole. On such a test, no society, past, present or future, can be anything but irresponsible. That is hardly worth saying explicitly, but it is worth pointing out that underneath such a procedure there is a confusion of moral categories, between political responsibility in the sense of a systematic pursuit of accepted public goals within the contemporaneous moral framework and modern notions of decency or humaneness. It is not inconsistent for an historian to judge a past action or behaviour to have been politically responsible and at the same time to condemn its moral underpinning.

I do not imply that political (or civic) responsibility was to be found in antiquity only in the democracies. Oligarchies and even despotisms could also act responsibly; but then, as in Rome, the assessment must be restricted to those who shared in the decision-making; of the others, the *demos*, the plebs, only obedience was expected, which the ruling class called responsible behaviour. And the Roman *demos* was remarkably obedient most of the time. Why? More specifically, why, once they had gained a measure of what Bosanquet called 'juristic liberty', did they not make a determined, sustained effort to obtain 'political liberty', or at least a greater share of it? The same question can, of course, be asked of many societies, but of few in which the obedient populace made up the armed forces not through hire or impressment but as a citizen's obligation. Rome's unique military history itself provides some of the answer, as we have seen, but for the decisive element we must look to the ideology, the whole complex of beliefs and attitudes which have been a leitmotiv of this book. The ideology of a ruling class is of little use unless it is accepted by those who are being ruled, and so it was to an extraordinary degree in Rome. Then, when the ideology began to disintegrate within the élite itself, the consequence was not to broaden the political liberty among the citizenry but, on the contrary, to destroy it for everyone.

BIBLIOGRAPHY

Note: Works cited only once are not normally repeated here.

Astin, A. E. (1967). *Scipio Aemilianus.* Oxford

Astin, A. E. (1968). *Politics and Policies in the Roman Republic* (an inaugural lecture). Belfast

Astin, A. E. (1978). *Cato the Censor.* Oxford

Badian, E., ed. (1966). *Ancient Society and Institutions. Studies Presented to Victor Ehrenberg.* Oxford

Badian, E. (1972). 'Tiberius Gracchus and the Beginning of the Roman Revolution', in *Aufstieg und Niedergang der römischen Welt,* ed. H. Temporini, I 1, 668–731. Berlin

Brunt, P. A. (1971a). *Social Conflicts in the Roman Republic.* London

Brunt, P. A. (1971b). *Italian Manpower 225 B.C. – A.D. 14.* Oxford

Brunt, P. A. (forthcoming). 'The Roman Clientela: A Reconsideration'

Connor, W. R. (1968). *Theopompus and Fifth-Century Athens.* Washington

Connor, W. R. (1971). *The New Politicians of Fifth-Century Athens.* Princeton

Davies, J. K. (1971). *Athenian Propertied Families 600–300 B.C.* Oxford

de Ste Croix, G. E. M. (1972). *The Origins of the Peloponnesian War.* London

Dunn, John (1980). *Political Obligation in Its Historical Context.* Cambridge

Ehrenberg, V. (1965). *Polis und Imperium,* ed. K. F. Stroheker and A. J. Graham. Zurich & Stuttgart

Ehrenberg, V. (1976). *L'état grec,* trans. C. Picavet-Roos, ed. Ed. Will (the latest ed. of a book originally publ. in German in 1932). Paris

Ferguson W. S. (1911). *Hellenistic Athens.* London

Finley, M. I. (1962). 'Athenian Demagogues', *Past & Present* 21: 3–24, reprinted in and cited from *Studies in Ancient Society,* ed. Finley (London & Boston 1974) 1–25

Finley, M. I. (1973a). *The Ancient Economy.* Berkeley & London

Finley, M. I. (1973b). *Democracy Ancient and Modern.* New Brunswick, N. J. & London

Finley, M. I. (1975). *The Use and Abuse of History.* London & New York

Finley, M. I. (1976a). 'The Freedom of the Citizen in the Greek World', *Talanta* 7: 1–23, repr. in Finley (1981) ch. 5

Finley, M. I., ed. (1976*b*). *Studies in Roman Property*. Cambridge

Finley, M. I. (1977). 'Censorship in Classical Antiquity', *Times Literary Supplement* for 27 July; in French, *Revue historique* 263 (1980) 3–20

Finley, M. I. (1978*a*). 'Empire in the Greco-Roman World', *Greece & Rome* 25: 1–15, repr. in *Review* 2: 55–68

Finley, M. I. (1978*b*). 'The Fifth-Century Athenian Empire: A Balance Sheet', in Garnsey/Whittaker (1978) 103–26, repr. in Finley (1981) ch. 3

Finley, M. I. (1979). *Ancient Sicily*, rev. ed. London

Finley, M. I. (1981). *Economy and Society in Ancient Greece*, ed. B. D. Shaw & R. P. Saller. London & New York

Fowler, W. W. (1911). *The Religious Experience of the Roman People*. London

Garlan, Y. (1975). *War in the Ancient World: A Social History*, trans. J. Lloyd. London

Garnsey, P. D. A. & Whittaker, C. R., ed. (1978). *Imperialism in the Ancient World*. Cambridge

Gauthier, P. (1974). '"Générosité" romaine et "avarice" grecque; sur l'octroi du droit de cité, in *Mélanges . . . William Seston* 207–15. Paris

Gehrke, H.-J. (1978). 'Das Verhältnis von Politik und Philosophie im Wirken des Demetrios von Phaleron', *Chiron* 8: 149–93

Goody, J. R., ed. (1968). *Literacy in Traditional Societies*. Cambridge

Grossmann, G. (1950). *Politische Schlagwörter aus der Zeit des Peloponnesischen Krieges*, repr. New York 1973. Diss. Zurich

Harris, W. V. (1979). *War and Imperialism in Republican Rome 327–70 B.C.* Oxford

Haussoullier, B. (1883). *La vie municipale en Attique*, repr. New York 1979. Paris

Headlam, J. W. (1933). *Election by Lot at Athens*, 2 ed. by D. G. Macgregor. Cambridge

Heuss, A. (1973). 'Das Revolutionsproblem im Spiegel der antiken Geschichte', *Historische Zeitschrift* 216: 1–72

Hignett, C. (1952). *A History of the Athenian Constitution to the End of the Fifth Century B.C.* Oxford

Hintze, O. (1962). *Staat und Verfassung*, 2 ed. by G. Oestreich. Göttingen

Hintze, O. (1964). *Soziologie und Geschichte*, 2 ed. by G. Oestreich. Göttingen

Hopkins, K. (1978). *Conquerors and Slaves*. Cambridge

Jocelyn, H. D. (1966/7). 'The Roman Nobility and the Religion of the Republican State', *Journal of Religious History* 4: 89–104

Kelly, J. M. (1966). *Roman Litigation*. Oxford

Kluwe, E. (1976). 'Die soziale Zusammensetzung der athenischen Ekklesia und ihr Einfluss auf politische Entscheidungen', *Klio* 58: 295–333

Kluwe, E. (1977). 'Nochmals zum Problem: Die soziale Zusammensetz-
    ung der athenischen Ekklesia . . .', *Klio* 59: 45–81
Kroll, W. (1933). *Die Kultur der ciceronischen Zeit*, 2 vols. Leipzig (repr.
    in one volume, Darmstadt 1963)
Lanza, D. (1979). *Lingua e discorso nell' Atene delle professioni.* Naples
Laski, H. J. (1935). *The State in Theory and Practice.* London
Laslett, P., ed. (1956). *Philosophy, Politics and Society.* Oxford
Liebeschuetz, J. W. G. (1979). *Continuity and Change in Roman Religion.*
    Oxford
Lintott, A. W. (1968). *Violence in Republican Rome.* Oxford
Lintott, A. W. (1982). *Violence, Civil Strife and Revolution in the Classical
    City.* London & Canberra
Loenen, D. (1953). *Stasis* (an inaugural lecture). Amsterdam
Lübtow, U. v. (1948). 'De iustitia et iure', *Zeitschrift der Savigny-Stiftung
    für Rechtsgeschichte. Romanistische Abt.* 66: 458–565
MacIntyre, A. (1981). *After Virtue, a Study in Moral Theory.* London
Meier, C. (1980). *Die Entstehung des Politischen bei den Griechen.* Frank-
    furt.
Meiggs, R. & Lewis, D., ed. (1969). *A Selection of Greek Historical
    Inscriptions to the End of the Fifth Century B.C.* Oxford
Merquior, J. G. (1980). *Rousseau and Weber: Two Studies in the Theory of
    Legitimacy.* London & Boston
Meyer, Ernst (1961). *Römischer Staat und Staatsgedanke*, 2 ed. Zurich &
    Stuttgart
Michels, A. K. (1967). *The Calendar of the Roman Republic.* Princeton
Mommsen, T. (1887–8). *Römisches Staatsrecht*, 3 ed., 3 vols. in 5. Leipzig
Mommsen, T. (1899). *Römisches Strafrecht*, cited from the 1961 photo-
    graphic reprint. Darmstadt
Nicolet, C. (1970). 'Cicéron, Platon et le vote secret', *Historia* 19: 39–66
Nicolet, C. (1976). *Le métier de citoyen dans la Rome républicaine.* Paris
    (trans. P. S. Falla, London 1980)
Nippel, W. (1980). *Mischverfassungstheorie und Verfassungsrealität in
    Antike und früher Neuzeit.* Stuttgart
Pöhlmann, R. (1925). *Geschichte der sozialen Frage und des Sozialismus in
    der antiken Welt*, 2 vols., 3 ed. by F. Oertel. Munich
Pritchett, W. K. (1971–9). *The Greek State at War*, 3 vols. Berkeley
Rhodes, P. J. (1972). *The Athenian Boule.* Oxford
Rhodes, P. J. (1980). 'Ephebai, Bouleutae and the Population of Athens',
    Zeitschrift für Papyrologie und Epigraphik 38: 191–201
Riepl. W. (1913). *Das Nachrichtenwesen des Altertums, mit besonderer
    Rücksicht auf die Römer.* Leipzig & Berlin
Roussel, D. (1976). *Tribu et Cité* (Annales littéraires de l'Univ. de
    Besançon 193)
Ryffel, H. (1949). *Metabole Politeion. Der Wandel der Staatsverfassungen.*
    Bern (repr. New York 1973)

Schmidt, S. W., et al., ed. (1977). *Friends, Followers, and Factions: A Reader in Political Clientalism*. Berkeley

Schuller, W. (1979). 'Zur Entstehung der griechischen Demokratie ausserhalb Athens', in *Auf den Weg gebracht*, ed. H. Sund & M. Timmermann 433–47. Konstanz

Scott, J. C. (1977). 'Patronage or Eploitation?', in *Patrons and Clients in Mediterranean Societies*, ed. E. Gellner & J. Waterbury 21–39. London

Spahn, P. (1977). *Mittelschicht und Polisbildung*. Frankfurt

Starr, C. G. (1974). *Political Intelligence in Classical Greece* (*Mnemosyne*, Supp. 31)

Staveley, E. S. (1972). *Greek and Roman Voting and Elections*. London

Strasburger, H. (1982). *Studien zur alten Geschichte*, 2 vols., ed. W. Schmitthenner and R. Zoepffel. Hildesheim & New York

Syme, R. (1939). *The Roman Revolution*. Oxford

Taylor, L. R. (1949). *Party Politics in the Age of Caesar* (cited from the paperback 1961). Berkeley

Taylor, L. R. (1960). *The Voting Districts of the Roman Republic* (Papers and Monographs of the American Academy in Rome 20)

Taylor, L. R. (1966). *Roman Voting Assemblies*. Ann Arbor

Traill, J. S. (1975). *The Political Organization of Attica* (*Hesperia*, Supp. 14)

Ungern-Sternberg von Pürkel, J. (1970). *Untersuchungen zum spätrepublikanischen Notstandsrecht*. Munich

Veyne, P. (1976). *Le pain et le cirque. Sociologie historique d'un pluralisme politique*. Paris

Vlastos, G. (1977). 'The Theory of Social Justice in the *Polis* in Plato's *Republic*', in *Interpretations of Plato*, ed. H. F. North 1–40. Leiden

Weber, M. (1972). *Wirtschaft und Gesellschaft*, 5 ed. by J. Winckelmann. Tübingen

INDEX

Achaean League, 116, 127
Acragas, 103
aediles, 39, 90
Aegina, 103
Aeschines, 37, 83, 136n
Aetolian League, 116
Agis IV, King of Sparta, 103, 116
Alcibiades, 54, 68, 94, 101, 118, 122, 134
Alexander III (the Great) of Macedonia, 12, 116
Andocides, 21
Antipater, 16
Antony, Mark, 117
Appian, 4, 21, 90
archons, 102, 107
Areopagus, Council of the, 71, 102
Arginusae, 140
Argos, 22n, 103, 108–9
Aristides, 50, 55, 67
aristocrats, aristocracy, 3; as term, 12; and wealth, 13–15; in Mantinea, 42; as 'tribal chieftains', 44–7; and leadership, 47; and rule in Rome, 137; see also class; élite
Aristophanes, 82, 123; Acharnians, 125; Clouds, 28
Aristotle: and class, 2, 10–11; on state, 6; and acceptance of political order, 27; on oligarchs, 39; and community patronage, 39–40; and Cleisthenes' reforms, 44; on Carthage, 53; on Spartan kings and ephors, 62; and Athens Assembly, 73, 75; and political analysis, 124, 126; and ideology, 132, 135; on equality, 137; Constitution of Athens, 39, 40, 47, 72, 102–4, 107; Constitutions (lost), 103; Politics: on class, 1, 3, 9–11; on to meson, 10; on political man, 24–5; and public service, 35; on Carthage, 53; on separation of powers, 58; on oligarchies, 63; on constitutional crises, 101; and political analysis, 124;

and rule, 137; Rhetoric, 29, 71, 75
army, armies, 17–18, 21–2, 58–9, 66–8, 129; see also militia; war; and individual city-states
Assembly (Athens), 56, 71–8, 80–4, 86, 90, 137, 139–40
Astin, A. E., 92, 97–8, 100
Athens: class in, 2, 13, 16; as city-state, 15, 17, 62–3; and citizenship, 15, 71; foreign domination and settlement, 16–17, 61, 63, 111, 113–14; military forces, 19, 130n; police and peace-keeping, 21; and invasion of Sicily, 21, 94, 113, 122; stability and continuity, 24–5, 49, 84, 106; class and political order in, 27, 31; land hunger, 33; state support for poor, 38, 40; liturgies, 36; public celebrations, 39; political participation, 40; Cleisthenes' reforms, 42–4, 46–8, 102, 115, 131; aristocratic rule, 46–7; destroyed by Macedon, 49, 116–17; ostracism, 50, 55; political procedures, 50–1, 54; and constitutional law, 56; political institutions, 56–8, 63; size, 59, 63; wars, 60; political and military leadership, 67–8; Assembly and Councils, 70–84, 86, 90, 107, 137, 139–40; war with Sparta, 73, 113, 122, 125; and Philip of Macedon, 78–81, 115; corruption in, 83–4; political consciousness, 97; constitutional conflict and change, 101, 107; and debt, 109; conservatism and 'decline', 115–16; political analysis in, 123–5, 129; ideology, 131, 133; rule by demos, 134–5, 140; and equality, 139–40; see also Greece; Peloponnesian War; Pisistratus
Attica, 16, 45, 63, 74
Atticus, Titus Pomponius, 43, 51
auctoritas, 8, 32, 43, 139
augurs see divination

INDEX

Roussel, Denis, 45

sacramentum, 130
'Sacred Band' (Thebes), 19
Sallust, 22, 128
Samos, 103, 109
Saturninus, 4, 117
Scipio Aemilianus, 91, 112, 127–8
Scipio Nasica, 5
Senate (Rome): and republic, 4–7; and civil disorder, 21; powers, 25, 52, 56; service in, 58; membership, 88; and popular opposition, 91–2; and divination, 102; and effect of elections, 98; and Bacchanalians, 100; and policy, 114; incompetents in, 140
senatus consultum ultimum, 3–6, 130
Servius Tullius, King of Rome, 115
Shklar, Judith, 70
Sicily: Athenian expedition to, 21, 94, 113, 122; as Roman province, 33; Greek communities in, 53; and conquest, 61
silver mines, 16
slaves: and social structure, 9; rights of freed, 17–18; as police, 20; in city-states, 41; political exclusion, 84; and Roman citizenship, 87; freeing of, 109; and free men, 138
Socrates, 28, 52, 67, 76, 125, 129n, 135
Solon: on class, 1–2, 13, 46; Dionysius on, 12; and law codes, 30; reforms, 40, 102; establishes first Athens council, 57; and debts, 107, 109; and stasis, 111n
Sophists, 28, 123, 132
Sophocles: Antigone, 125
sovereignty, 7–8
Sparta: as city state, 12, 62; foreign territorial domination and settlement, 16, 71, 106, 111; class in, 16; military service, 19; stability, 24, 106; and education, 28; and Mantinea, 42–3; military successes, 49; political institutions, 57; and power of military, 58–9; size, 59; political system and leadership, 59–60, 62, 66; wars and military activities, 60, 129–30; citizenship, 62; war with Athens, 73, 113, 122, 125; constitutional changes, 103; supremacy and decline, 116; and Rome, 129–30; ideology, 131

speech, freedom of, 29, 139
stasis, 4; Aristotle on, 10, 105–6, 108–9, 111, 116; and allegiance, 123; in Rome, 129, 134; and legitimacy, 133; and rule by law, 136
state, the: Roman, 3; Aristotle on, 6; and government, 7–9, 18; support for poor, 33–4; and politics, 51–2; and legitimacy, 122–3
Stoics, 128
strategoi, 57–8, 67, 71n, 78n, 102, 140
subversion (and civil disorder), 21–2, 24; see also civil war
Sulla, 59, 117, 120
sumptuary laws, 100
Syme, R., 119, 121
Syracuse, 103, 126n

Tables, XII (Rome), 107
taxation, 32–3
Taylor, Lily Ross, 89, 118
Thebes, 16, 19, 79, 103, 116
Themistocles, 1, 50, 55, 115
Thera, 110n
Theseus, 102, 133, 136, 138–9
Thessaly, 16
Thirty, tyranny of the, 102
Thucydides: and politics, 54; on Corcyra, 61; on Cleon, 67; on popular participation, 73, 75, 80; and Assembly, 76, 81–2; and Eleusinian protest, 94; on oligarchic coup, 102; on constitutional changes, 103; on Nicias and Sicilian expedition, 113; and Alcibiades, 122; political analysis in, 123; on fear and illegal acts, 134
Timaeus: History, 103
timouchoi, 104
treason, 122–3
tribe, tribes, 45–8, 53, 85, 87, 90
tribunes (Rome), 86, 99, 107
tribute, 32, 76–7
triumphs (formal), 66, 90, 95
tumultus, 22n
tyranny, tyrants, 1, 4, 32, 61, 101, 111, 129; see also Pisistratus

urbanization, 60

veto, 53, 86
Veyne, P., 39
violence (armed), 4–5
Vlastos, G., 126